The Bible and I

Being Noonday
With Business Men on
Faith and Unbelief

By

R. A. TORREY

Author oj

" What the Bible Teaches," " How to Pray," etc.

NEW YORK   CHICAGO   TORONTO

Fleming H. Revell Company

LONDON AND EDINBURGH

Copyright 1904-1906, by
FLEMING H. REVELL COMPANY

New York: 158 Fifth Avenue
Chicago: 17 North Wabash Ave.
London: 21 Paternoster Square
Edinburgh: 75 Princes Street

Printing Statement:

Due to the very old age and scarcity of this book,
many of the pages may be hard to read due to the
blurring of the original text, possible missing pages,
missing text and other issues beyond our control.

Because this is such an important and rare work, we
believe it is best to reproduce this book regardless of
its original condition.

Thank you for your understanding.

CONTENTS

		PAGE
I.	ONE REASON WHY I BELIEVE THE BIBLE TO BE THE WORD OF GOD	1
II.	TWO MORE REASONS WHY I BELIEVE THE BIBLE TO BE THE WORD OF GOD . . .	17
III.	FOUR MORE REASONS WHY I BELIEVE THE BIBLE TO BE THE WORD OF GOD	29
IV.	THREE MORE REASONS WHY I BELIEVE THE BIBLE TO BE THE WORD OF GOD . .	43
V	DID JESUS CHRIST REALLY RISE FROM THE DEAD ?	58
VI.	THE SELF-EVIDENT TRUTHFULNESS OF THE GOSPEL STORIES OF THE RESURRECTION . .	70
VII.	THE CIRCUMSTANTIAL EVIDENCE OF THE RESURRECTION OF CHRIST	86
VIII.	WHAT THE RESURRECTION OF JESUS FROM THE DEAD PROVES	101
IX.	INFIDELITY : ITS CAUSES, CONSEQUENCES, AND CURE	112
X.	INFIDELITY : ITS CONSEQUENCES AND CURE .	125

INTRODUCTION

THE addresses in this book have been delivered to large audiences of business and professional men in cities and large towns in Australia, New Zealand, Tasmania, England, Scotland, and Ireland. Many who have been helped by them have urged me to put them into book form in order that they may be preserved for reference, and that they may be circulated among friends, hence this volume.

In Melbourne the Town Hall was packed with 2500 men of all classes at the noon hour each day to listen to these addresses. In Sydney I am told that in the crowd that thronged the Centenary Hall there were many prominent business men and members of both Houses of the Legislature, who gave up their mid-day meal each day to attend. In Great Britain and Ireland men very prominent in commercial and professional life, a large number of University men, both professors and students, have spoken to me of the help that has come to them from these addresses, not a few having been shaken in their faith by the critical discussions of the present day. Many agnostics, skeptics, Unitarians, and destructive critics have testified publicly to having been led by these lectures to give up their former erroneous positions. I have been especially encouraged by the number of my brethren in the ministry who have testified in public and private of the help received. I pray that these addresses may be used in this printed form to lead many thousands more out into the light and strength that come from faith in the Bible and in the Christ of the Bible.

FIRST TALK

THE most important question in religious thought is, "Is the Bible the Word of God?" If the Bible is the Word of God, an absolutely trustworthy revelation from God Himself of Himself, His purposes and His will, of man's duty and destiny of spiritual and eternal realities, then we have a starting-point from which we can proceed to the conquest of the whole domain of religious truth. But if the Bible is not the Word of God, if it is the mere product of man's thinking, speculating, and guessing, not altogether trustworthy in regard to religious and eternal truth, then we are all at sea, not knowing whither we are drifting, but we may be sure that we are not drifting toward any safe port.

I did not always believe the Bible to be the Word of God. I sincerely doubted that the Bible was the Word of God. I doubted that Jesus Christ was the Son of God. I doubted whether there was a personal God. I was not an infidel—I was a skeptic. I did not deny—I questioned. I was not an atheist—I was an agnostic. I did not know, but I determined to find out. If there was a God, I determined to find that out, and act accordingly. If there was not a God, I determined to find that out, and act accordingly. If Jesus Christ was the Son of God, I determined to find that out, and act accordingly. If Jesus Christ was not the Son of God, I determined to find that out, and act accordingly. If the Bible was the Word of God, I determined to find that out, and act accordingly; and if the Bible was not the Word of God, I determined to find that out, and act accordingly. I found out. I found out beyond a peradventure that there is a God, that Jesus Christ is the Son of God, that the Bible is the Word of God. To-day it is with me not a matter of mere probability, nor even of mere belief, but of absolute certainty.

I am going to give you some of the reasons why I believe the Bible to be the Word of God. Not all the reasons—it would take months to do that; not even the reasons which are most conclusive to me personally, for these are of such a personal and experimental character that they cannot be conveyed to another. But I will give you reasons that will prove conclusive to any candid seeker after the truth, to anyone who desires to know the truth and is willing to obey it. They will not convince one who is determined not to know the truth, or who is unwilling to obey it. If one will not receive the love of the truth, he must be left to his own deliberate choice of error, and given over to strong delusion to believe a lie. But if one is searching for the truth, no matter how completely he is in the fog to-day, he can be led into the truth.

I believe the Bible to be the Word of God, first of all, because of the testimony of Jesus Christ to that fact. We live in a day in which many men say that they accept the teaching of Jesus Christ, but that they do not accept the teaching of the whole Bible; that they believe what Jesus Christ says, but as to what Moses said, or is said to have said, and what Isaiah said, or is said to have said, and what Jeremiah said, and Paul said, and John said, and the rest of the Bible writers, they do not know about that. This position may at the first glance seem rational, but, in point of fact, it is utterly irrational. If we accept the teaching of Jesus Christ, we must accept the whole Bible, for Jesus Christ has set His stamp of His authority upon the entire Book, and if we accept His authority, we must accept all that upon which He sets the stamp of His authority.

As to Christ's endorsement of the Old Testament, turn first of all to Mark vii. 13. Jesus has just quoted from the Law of Moses, not merely from the Ten Commandments, but from other portions of the Law of Moses as well. He has set over against the teaching of the Law of Moses the traditions of the Pharisees and Scribes, and in this verse He says, You do make "*the Word of God* of none effect throughout your tradition." Here He distinctly calls the Law of Moses the " Word of God." It is oftentimes said that the Bible nowhere claims to be the Word of God. Here Jesus Christ Himself distinctly asserts that the Law of Moses is the Word of God. If, then, we accept the authority of Jesus Christ, we must accept the Law of Moses as "the Word of God." Of course this only covers the first five books of the Old Testament, but if we can accept this as the Word of God, we will have little difficulty with the rest of the Old Testament, for it is here that the hottest battle is being fought to-day.

Turn again to Matthew v. 18. Here Jesus says, " Till heaven and earth pass away, one jot or one tittle shall in nowise pass from the law until all be fulfilled." Now every Hebrew scholar knows that a " jot " is the Hebrew character " yodh," the smallest character in the Hebrew alphabet, less than half the size of any other character in the Hebrew alphabet, and that a " tittle " is a little horn that the Hebrews put on their consonants; and here Jesus asserts that the Law of Moses as originally given is absolutely infallible down to its smallest letter and part of a letter. If, then, we accept the authority of Jesus Christ, we must accept the authority of the Law of Moses as originally given, and as contained in the Old Testament Scriptures.

Turn next to John x. 35. Jesus has just

quoted in proof of a point which He is making from one of the Psalms, and adds, "The Scripture cannot be broken," thus setting the stamp of His authority upon the absolute irrefragability of the Old Testament Scriptures. Turn again to Luke xxiv. 27, and you will read that Jesus, "Beginning at Moses and all the prophets, expounded unto them *in all the Scriptures* the things concerning Himself"; and in the 44th verse He says, "All things must be fulfilled which were written in the Law of Moses, and in the prophets, and in the Psalms." Now every scholar knows that the Jews divided their Bible (our present Old Testament Scriptures) into three parts: the law (the first five books of the Old Testament); the prophets (most of the books which we call prophetic, and some of those which we call historical); and the remaining books of the Old Testament, the Psalms or Sacred Writings. Jesus Christ takes up each one of these three recognized divisions of these Old Testament Scriptures and sets the stamp of His authority upon each of them. If, then we accept the authority of Jesus Christ, we are driven logically to accept the entire Old Testament Scriptures.

In Luke xvi. 31 Jesus says, "If they hear not Moses and the prophets, neither will they be persuaded though one be raised from the dead," thus in the most emphatic way indorsing the truth of the Old Testament Scriptures.

In John v. 47 He says, " If ye believe not his
[Moses'] writings, how shall ye believe My
words?" thus setting the stamp of His authority
upon the teaching of Moses as being as truly
from God as was His own. We must then, if
we accept the authority of Jesus Christ, accept
the entire Old Testament.

But how about the New Testament? Did
Jesus set the stamp of His authority upon it also?
He did. But how could He when not a book of
the New Testament was written when He de-
parted from this earth? By way of anticipation.
Turn to John xiv. 26 and you will hear Jesus
saying, " The Comforter, which is the Holy
Ghost, whom the Father will send in My name,
He shall teach you all things and bring all things
to your remembrance whatsoever I have said
unto you," thus setting the stamp of His authority, not only upon the Apostolic teaching as
given by the Holy Ghost, but upon the Apostolic
recollection of what He Himself had taught.
The question is often asked, " How do we know
that in the Gospel records we have an accurate
reproduction of the teaching of Jesus Christ?"
It is asked, " Did the Apostles take notes at the
time of what Jesus said?" There is reason to
believe that they did, that Matthew and Peter,
from whom Mark derived his material, and
James (from whom, there is reason to believe,
Luke obtained much of his material) took notes
of what Jesus said in Aramaic, and that John

took notes of what Jesus said in Greek, and that
we have in the four Gospels the report of what
they took down at the time. But whether this be
true or not does not matter for our present
purposes, for we have Christ's own authority
for it that in the Apostolic records we have not
the Apostles' recollection of what Jesus said,
but the Holy Ghost's recollection of what Jesus
said, and, while the Apostles might forget and
report inaccurately, the Holy Ghost could not
forget.

Turn furthermore to John xvi. 12, 13, and you
will hear Jesus saying, " I have yet many things
to say unto you, but ye cannot bear them now.
Howbeit when He, the Spirit of truth, is come,
He will guide you into all truth." Here Jesus
sets the stamp of His authority upon the teaching of the Apostles as being given by the Holy
Ghost, as containing all the truth, and as containing more truth than His own teaching. He tells
the Apostles that He has many things that He
knows to tell them, but that they are not ready
yet to receive them, but that when the Holy
Spirit comes, He will guide them into this fuller
and larger truth. If then we accept the authority of Jesus Christ, we must accept the Apostolic teaching, the New Testament writings, as
being given through the Holy Spirit, as containing all the truth, and as containing more truth
than Jesus taught while on earth. There are
many in our day crying, " Back to Christ," by

which they usually mean, " We do not care what Paul taught, or what John taught, or what James taught, or what Jude taught. We do not know about them. Let us go back to Christ, the original source of authority, and accept what He taught, and that alone." Very well, " Back to Christ." The cry is not a bad one, but when you get back to Christ, you hear Christ Himself saying, " On to the Apostles. They have more truth to teach than I have taught. The Holy Spirit has taught them all the truth. Listen to them." If then we accept the authority of Jesus Christ, we are driven to accept the authority of the entire New Testament.

So then if we accept the teaching of Jesus Christ, we must accept the entire Old Testament and the entire New Testament. It is either Christ and the whole Bible, or no Bible and no Christ. There are some in these days who say that they believe in Christ, but not in the Christ of the New Testament. But there is no Christ but the Christ of the New Testament. Any other Christ than the Christ of the New Testament is a pure figment of the imagination. Any other Christ than the Christ of the New Testament is an idol made by man's own fancy, and whoever worships him is an idolator. But we must accept the authority of Jesus Christ. He is accredited to us by five unmistakable divine testimonies.

First, by the testimony of the divine life that

He lived, for He lived as never man lived. Let any man take the four Gospels for himself and read them carefully and candidly, he will soon be convinced of two things:—First, that he is reading the story of a life actually lived, that no man could have imagined the character there set forth unless the life had been actually lived, much less could four men have imagined a character, each one of the four making his own account of that character, not only consistent with itself, but consistent with the other three. To suppose that these four men who wrote the Gospels imagined the life here set forth would be to suppose a greater miracle than any recorded in the Gospels. He will see, in the second place, that the life here set forth is apart from all other human lives, that it stands by itself, that it is manifestly a divine life lived under human conditions. Napoleon Bonaparte was a good judge of men. He once said regarding the life of Jesus as recorded in the Gospels, which he had been reading, " I know men [and if he did not know men, who ever did?], and Jesus Christ was not a man." What he meant was, of course, that Jesus Christ was not a mere man.

Second, Jesus Christ is accredited to us by the divine words that He spoke. If anyone will study the teaching of Jesus Christ with candor and faithfulness, he will soon see that it has a character that distinguishes it from all other teaching ever uttered on earth.

Third, Jesus Christ was accredited to us by the divine works that He wrought, not only healing the sick, which many others have done, but cleansing the leper, opening the eyes of the blind, raising the dead, stilling the tempest by a word, turning water into wine, and feeding 5000 with five small loaves and two small fishes, which was a creative act. These miracles of power are clear credentials of a God-sent Teacher. We cannot study them candidly and not come to the same conclusion as Nicodemus did, " We know that Thou art a Teacher come from God, for no man can do these signs that Thou doest, except God be with him." Of course, we bear in mind the fact that strenuous efforts have been made to eliminate the supernatural element from the story of the life of Jesus Christ, but all these efforts have resulted in failure, and all similar efforts must result in failure. The most able effort of this kind that was ever made was that of David Strauss in his " Leben Jesu." David Strauss was a man of remarkable ability and gifts, a man of real and profound scholarship, a man of notable genius, a man of singular power of critical analysis, a man of indomitable perseverance and untiring industry. He brought to bear all the rare gifts of His richly endowed mind upon the story of the life of Jesus with the determination to discredit the miraculous element therein contained. He spent his best years and strength in this effort. If anyone

could have succeeded in such an effort, David
Strauss was the man, but he failed utterly. For
a time it seemed to many that he had succeeded
in his purpose, but when his life of Jesus was
itself submitted to rigid, critical analysis it fell
all to pieces, and to-day is utterly discredited,
and those who wish to eliminate the miraculous
element in the story of Jesus feel that they must
make the attempt anew, since the attempt of
David Strauss has come to nothing. Where
David Strauss failed, Ernest Renan tried again.
He had not, by any means, the ability and genius
of Strauss, but he was a man of brilliant genius,
of subtle imagination, of rare literary skill, of
singular adroitness and finesse. His "Life of
Christ" was read with interest and admiration
by many. The work was done with fascinating
skill. Some fancied that Ernest Renan had succeeded in his attempt, but his "Life of Jesus"
naturally enough was discredited even in a
shorter time than that of David Strauss. All
other attempts have met with a similar fate. It
is an attempt at the impossible. Let any candid
man take the life of Jesus and read it for himself with attention and care, and he will soon
discover that the life there pictured could not
have been imagined, but must have been really
lived; that the teachings reported as uttered by
Jesus are no fictitious teachings put into the
mouth of a fictitious person, but the real utter-
ances of a real person. He will also discover

that the character and the teaching set forth in
the Gospels are inextricably interwoven with the
stories of the miracles. He will find that if you
eliminate the miracles, the character and the
teaching disappear, that the character and the
teachings cannot be separated from the miraculous element without a violence of treatment
that no reasonable man will permit. To-day
this much at least is proven, that Jesus lived and
wrought substantially as is recorded in the four
Gospel records of His life. Personally, I believe that more than this is proven, but this is
enough for our present purpose. If Jesus lived
and wrought substantially as the Gospels record,
cleansing the lepers, opening the eyes of the
blind, raising the dead, stilling the tempest with
His word, feeding the 5000 with the five small
loaves and the two small fishes, then He bears
unmistakable credentials as a Teacher sent and
indorsed by God.

Fourth, Jesus Christ is also accredited to us
in the fourth place by His divine influence upon
all subsequent history. Jesus Christ was beyond peradventure one of three things: He was
either the son of God in a unique sense,—a divine
Person incarnate in human form,—or else He was
the most daring impostor that ever lived, or else
one of the most hopeless lunatics. That He
claimed to be the Son of God in a unique sense,
and that all men should honor Him even as they
honored the Father (John v. 23), and that He

and the Father were one (John x. 30), and he that had seen Him had seen the Father (John xiv. 9), of this there can be no honest doubt. He was then either the divine Person that He claimed to be, or the most daring impostor, or a most hopeless lunatic. Was His influence upon subsequent history the influence of a lunatic? No one but a lunatic would say so. Was His influence upon subsequent history the influence of an impostor? No one but one whose own heart was thoroughly cankered with deceit and fraud would think of saying so. Not an impostor, not a lunatic, we have only one alternative left—He was what He claimed to be, the Son of God.

Fifth, Jesus Christ is accredited to us by His resurrection from the dead. Later on I shall present to you the evidence for the resurrection of Jesus Christ. We will see the historic evidence for the resurrection of Christ is absolutely convincing in its character, that the resurrection of Jesus Christ from the dead is one of the best proven facts of history. But the resurrection of Christ is God's seal to Christ's claim. Jesus Christ claimed to be the Son of God. He was put to death for making that claim. Before being put to death He said that God would set His seal to the claim by raising Him from the dead. They killed Him; they laid Him in the sepulcher; they rolled a stone to the door of the sepulcher; they sealed that door with the Roman seal, which to break was death; and when the appointed hour of which Christ had spoken came, the breath of God swept through the sleeping clay, and Jesus rose triumphant over death, and God spoke more clearly than if He should speak from the open heavens to-day and say, " This is My beloved Son. Hear ye Him."

We must then, if we are honest, accept the authority of Jesus Christ; but, as already seen, if we accept the authority of Jesus Christ, we must accept the entire Old Testament and the entire New Testament as being the Word of God; *therefore I believe the Bible to be the Word of God because of the testimony of Jesus Christ to that effect.*

A school of criticism has arisen that assumes to set up its authority against the authority of Jesus Christ. They say, for example, " Jesus says that the 110th Psalm was by David, and was Messianic; but we say that the 110th Psalm is neither by David, nor is it Messianic." They ask us to give up the authority and infallibility of Jesus Christ and the Bible, and accept their authority and their infallibility in their place. Very well, but before doing it we demand their credentials. We do not yield to the claim of authority and infallibility of anyone until he presents his credentials. Jesus Christ presents His credentials. First of all, He presents the credential of the divine life that He lived. What have they to place in comparison with that? We

hear much about the beauty of the life of some of
this school of critics. We have no desire to deny
the claim, but against the beauty of their lives we
put the life of Jesus. Which suffers by the comparison? If there is any force in the argument,
" If a man's life is in the right, his doctrine cannot be in the wrong "—and there is force in the
argument—it bears immeasurably more for the
authority of Jesus Christ than it does for the
authority of any critic or school of critics.

Second, Jesus presents the credential of the
divine words that He spoke. What have they
to put up against that? The words of Jesus
Christ have stood the test of eighteen centuries,
and shine out with greater luster and glory
to-day than ever. What school of criticism
has ever stood the test of eighteen years? If
one has to choose between the teaching of Christ
and that of any school of criticism, it will not
take any thoroughly sane man long to choose.

Third, Jesus Christ presents His third credential, the divine works that He wrought, the unmistakable seal of God upon His claims. What
has this school of criticism to put up against
that? Absolutely nothing. It has no miracles
but miracles of literary ingenuity in the attempt
to make the preposterous appear historical.

Fourth, Jesus Christ presents the credential
of His influence upon human history. We all
know what the influence of Jesus Christ has
been, how benign and how divine. Everything

that is best in modern civilization, everything that is best in national, domestic, and individual life, is due to the influence of Jesus Christ. Alas! we also know the influence of this school of criticism. We know that it is weakening the power of ministers and Christian workers everywhere. We know that it is emptying churches. We know that it is depleting missionary treasuries. We know that it is paralyzing missionary effort in every field where it has gone. I know this by personal observation, and not by hearsay. This may not be their intention. With some of them it is not their intention, but none the less it is a fact. The influence of Jesus has been thoroughly beneficent. The influence of this school of criticism is utterly bad.

Fifth, Jesus presents His fifth credential, His resurrection from the dead. What has this school of criticism to set up over against that? Nothing whatever. Jesus Christ establishes His claim. The opposing school of criticism stands dumb. Therefore we refuse to bow to the assumed and unsubstantiated authority and infallibility of any school of criticism, of any priest, or pope, or theological professor, but most gladly do we bow to the authority and infallibility of Jesus Christ, so completely proven, and upon His authority accept the entire Old Testament and the entire New Testament as the Word of God.

SECOND TALK

In the address of yesterday, we saw that if we accepted the authority of Jesus Christ we must accept the entire Old Testament and the entire New Testament, because He set the stamp of His authority on both; that it was either Christ and the whole Bible, or no Bible and no Christ. We saw, in the second place, that we must accept the authority of Jesus Christ because He was accredited to us by five unmistakably divine testimonies. First, the testimony of the divine life that he lived. Second, the testimony of the divine words that he spoke. Third, the testimony of the divine works that He wrought. Fourth, the testimony of His divine influence upon all subsequent history. Fifth, the testimony of His resurrection from the dead.

We saw, in the next place, that there was a school of criticism that assumed to set its authority up against that of Jesus Christ, that this school of criticism demanded that we should give up the infallibility of Christ and the Scriptures, and accept in the place of them the infallibility of this school of criticism. Before yielding to

17

their demand, we demanded their credentials. We saw that Jesus presented His credentials, which were convincing, but that this school of criticism had absolutely no credentials to present over against those of Jesus Christ. Therefore we refused to bow to their claim of authority and infallibility, but most gladly bowed to the fully proven authority and infallibility of Jesus Christ.

My second reason for believing the Bible to be the Word of God is because of its fulfilled prophecies. The average infidel knows absolutely nothing about fulfilled prophecy, and this is not to be wondered at, for the average Christian knows nothing about fulfilled prophecy, and even the average preacher knows practically nothing about fulfilled prophecy. The subject of prophecy is a large one, and to go into it thoroughly would take many days, but it can be presented in outline in a few moments with sufficient fullness to show the overwhelming weight of the argument. There are in the Bible two kinds of prophecy: first, the explicit verbal prophecies, and second, the prophecies of the types and symbols.

We will take up first the explicit verbal prophecies. These are of three kinds; first, prophecies regarding the coming Messiah; second, prophecies regarding the Jewish people; third, prophecies regarding the Gentile nations. We will limit ourselves this morning to prophecies regarding the coming Messiah, and take only five of them by way of illustration. Isaiah liii. (the entire chapter) ; Micah v. 2; Daniel ix. 25-27; Jeremiah xxiii. 5, 6; Psalms xvi. 8-11. In the passages cited we have predictions of a coming King of Israel. We are told the exact time of His manifestation to His people, the exact place of His birth, the family of which He should be born, the condition of the family at the time of His birth (a condition entirely different from that existing at the time the prophecy was written, and contrary to all the probabilities in the case), the manner of His reception by His people (a reception entirely different from that which would naturally be expected), the fact, method, and details regarding His death, with the specific circumstances regarding His burial, His resurrection subsequent to His burial, and His victory subsequent to His resurrection. These predictions were fulfilled with the most minute precision in Jesus of Nazareth.

An attempt has been made by the rationalists to show that Isaiah liii. does not refer to the coming Messiah. It is natural that they should attempt this, for if it does refer to the coming Messiah, the case of the rationalists is hopeless. That it does refer to the coming Messiah is evident from the fact that this chapter was taken to be Messianic by the Jews themselves until its fulfillment in Jesus of Nazareth, and their unwillingness to accept Him as the Messiah drove

them into the attempt to show that it was not
Messianic. Furthermore, the desperate straits
to which those who deny its Messianic applica-
tion are driven show the hopelessness of their
case. When asked who the suffering One of
Isaiah liii. is, if He is not the Messiah, the best
answer they can get is that it refers to suffering
Israel; but anyone who will carefully read the
passage will see that this interpretation is impossible. The sufferer of Isaiah liii. is represented as suffering for the sins of others than
Himself, and those for whom He is suffering
are represented as " My people," that is, Israel
(verse 8). Now, if the sufferer is suffering for
sins of others than Himself, and the others than
Himself for whom He is suffering are Israel,
then surely the sufferer Himself cannot be
Israel.

You can bring the prophecies cited down to
the very latest date to which the most daring
destructive critic ever thought of assigning them,
and still they are hundreds of years before the
birth of Jesus of Nazareth. How are we going
to account for it, that this Book has the power of
looking into the future hundreds of years and
predicting with most minute precision things to
come to pass then, and that these predictions are
fulfilled to the very letter? Facts demanding
accounting for. You are business men—theologians may weave their theories out of their own
inner consciousness without regard to facts, but

business men must face facts, and here are facts. There is but one rational explanation of it. Any book that has the power of looking hundreds of years into the future, and predicting with minute precision as to person, place, time, circumstances, detailed things to occur at that remote period, must have for its author the only person in the universe who knows the end from the beginning —that is God. Of course, it is quite possible for a far-seeing man to look a few years into the future, and, by studying causes now operant, predict in a general way some things that will occur. But this is not at all our problem with the Bible. It is not a few years into the future, but hundreds of years into the future; not in a general way, but with minute and specific fullness. It is not of things the causes of which are now operant and discernible, but things the causes of which are not discernible at the present time, and these predictions fulfilled to the letter. To a mind willing to bow to facts and their necessary meaning, it is conclusive evidence of the Divine origin of the Book.

A noteworthy fact regarding the prophecies of the Bible is that oftentimes there are two seemingly contradictory lines of prophecy, and it seems as though if the one line of prophecy were fulfilled, the other could not be; and yet these two seemingly contradictory lines of prophecy will converge and be fulfilled in one Person. For example, in the Old Testament we have two

lines of prophecy concerning the Messiah; one
line predicts a suffering Messiah, " despised and
rejected of men," " a man of sorrows and ac-
quainted with grief," whose earthly mission
should end in death and ignominy. The other
line of prophecy predicts with equal clearness
and definiteness an all-conquering Messiah, who
should rule the nations with a rod of iron. How
can both of these lines of prophecy be true? The
best answer the ancient Jew had, before the fulfillment of both lines in Christ, was that there
were to be two Messiahs, one a suffering Messiah of the tribe of Joseph, and one a con-
quering Messiah of the tribe of Judah; but in the
actual fulfillment both lines of prophecy meet in
the one Person, Jesus of Nazareth, who at His
first coming is the suffering Messiah, making
atonement for sin by His death upon the cross,
as so often predicted in the Old Testament, and
at His second coming He will come as a con-
quering King to rule the nations.

But the prophecies of the types and symbols
are even more conclusive than the explicit verbal
prophecies. If you ask the ordinary, superficial
student of the Bible, how much of the Old Testament is prophetical, he will reply something like
this, " Isaiah, Jeremiah, Ezekiel, Daniel, and the
Minor Prophets are prophetical," and may add
that there are also prophetical passages here and
there in the Psalms and Pentateuch. But if
you ask a thorough-going student of the Bible

how much of the Old Testament is prophetical, he will tell you that the entire book is prophetical, that its history is prophetical, that its personages are prophetical, that its institutions, ceremonies, offerings, and feasts are prophetical. If you are incredulous (as you have a right to be until you have investigated, but you have no right to remain incredulous unless you do investigate), but will take time, he will sit down and take you through the whole Book from the first chapter of Genesis to the last chapter of Malachi, and will show you everywhere unmistakable foreshadowings of things to come. He will show you in the lives of Abraham, Isaac, Joseph, David, and Solomon unquestionable foreshadowings of the truth regarding Christ. He will show you in every sacrifice and offering, in every feast, in every institution, in the tabernacle, and in every part of the tabernacle, its outer court, Holy Place and Most Holy Place, brazen altar, golden candlestick, table of shew bread, golden altar of incense, the veil that hung between the Holy Place and Most Holy Place, ark of the convenant, in its boards, bars, sockets and tenons, and the very coverings of the tabernacle, the clearest setting forth of every truth about Christ—His Person, His nature, His character, His atoning death, His resurrection, His ascension and coming again, and of all the facts of Jewish and Christian history. He will show you every profoundest truth which was to be fully revealed in the New Testament prefigured in the types and symbols of the Old Testament. At first, this very likely will seem to you like a mere happy coincidence, but as you go on verse after verse, chapter after chapter, book after book, if you are a fair-minded man, you will at last be overwhelmingly convinced that this was the thought and intention of the real author; and as you see in this ancient history, and in this legislation ordained to meet the immediate needs of the people, the setting forth of all the profoundest truths of Christian doctrine, and the perfect foreshadowing of all the facts of the history of Christ, the Jewish people and the Church, you will be driven to recognize in it the mind and wisdom of God. The modern critical theories regarding the construction of Exodus, Leviticus, Numbers, and Deuteronomy go all to pieces when considered in the light of the meaning of the types of the Old Testament. I have never known a destructive critic that knew anything to speak of regarding the types. One cannot study them thoroughly without being profoundly convinced that the real author of the Old Testament, back of the human authors, is God.

My third reason for believing the Bible to be the Word of God is because of the unity of the Book. This is an old argument, but a good one. The Bible is composed, as I suppose you know, of sixty-six parts or books. It is oftentimes said that the Bible is not a book, but a library. This is partly true, partly false. It is true the Bible is a library, but at the same time it is the most intensely one book of any book extant. The sixty-six books which compose the Bible were written by at least forty different authors. They were written in three different languages, Hebrew, Aramaic, and Greek. The period of their composition extends over at least 1500 years. They were written in countries hundreds of miles apart. They were written by men upon every plane of political and social life, from the king upon the throne down to the herdman and shepherd and fisherman and the petty politician. They display every form of literary structure. In the Bible we find all kinds of poetry, epic poetry, lyric poetry, didactic poetry, erotic poetry —elegy and rhapsody. We find all kinds of prose as well—historic prose, didactic prose, theological treatise, epistle, proverb, parable, allegory, and oration. In a book so composite, made up of such divergent parts, composed at such remote periods of time, and under such diverse circumstances, what would we naturally expect? Variance and discord, utter lack of unity. In point of fact, what do we find? The most marvellous unity. Every part of the Bible fits every other part of the Bible—one ever-increasing, ever-growing thought pervades the whole.

The character of this unity is most significant.

It is not a superficial unity, but a profound unity. On the surface, we often find apparent discrepancy and disagreement, but, as we study, the apparent discrepancy and disagreement disappear, and the deep underlying unity appears. The more deeply we study, the more complete do we find the unity to be.

The unity is also an organic one—that is, it is not the unity of a dead thing, like a stone, but of a living thing, like a plant. In the early books of the Bible we have the germinant thought; as we go on we have the plant, and further on the bud, and then the blossom, and then the ripened fruit. In Revelation we find the ripened fruit of Genesis.

How are we to account for it? Here is another fact that demands accounting for, and as business men you have to deal with facts, not theories; realities, and not fine-spun speculations of cloistered theologians, dreaming apart from the substantial realities of life. There is one easy and simple way of accounting for it, and only one rational way of accounting for it at all, and that is, that back of the forty or more human authors was the One all-governing, all-controlling, all-superintending, all-shaping mind of God.

Suppose it were proposed to build in our capital city in America, Washington, a temple that should represent the stone products of every State in the Union. The stones were to come

from every State in the Union; some from
the marble quarries of Marlboro, N. H., others
from the granite quarries of Quincy, Mass.,
some from the brownstone quarries of Mid-
dletown, Conn., some from the white marble
quarries at Rutland, Vt., some from the
gray sandstone quarries at Berea, Ohio, some
from the porphyry quarries below Knoxville,
Tenn., and some from the redstone quarries near
Hancock, Mich., some from the brownstone
quarries at Kasota, Minn., some from the
gypsum quarries of the Far West; some stones
from every State in the Union. The stones were
to be of all conceivable sizes and shapes—some
large, some small, some medium, some were to
be cubical, some spherical, some cylindrical,
some conical, some trapezoidal, and some rec-
tangular parallelopipedons. Each stone was to
be hewn into its final shape at the quarry from
which it was taken. Not a stone was to be
touched by mallet or chisel after it reached its
destination. Finally the stones are at Washington, and the builders go to work. As they build,
they find that every stone fits into every other
stone, and into its place. It is found that there
is not one stone too many, or one stone too few,
until at last the builders' work is done and there
rises before you a temple with its side walls, its
buttresses, its naves, its arches, its transepts and
its choirs, its roof, its pinnacles, and its dome,
perfect in every outline and in every detail, not

one stone too many and not one stone too few,
not one stone left over, and no niche or corner
where one stone is lacking, and yet every stone
hewn into its final shape in the quarry from
which it was taken. How would you account
for it? There is one very simple way to account
for it, and only one to account for it at all,
namely, that back of the individual quarrymen
was the master architect who planned the whole
building from the beginning and gave to each
individual quarryman his specifications for the
work. Now this is precisely what we find in
that temple of eternal truth which we call the
Bible, the stones for which were quarried in
places remote from one another by hundreds of
miles, and at periods of time 1500 years apart;
stones of all conceivable sizes and shapes, and
yet every stone fitting into its place and fitting
every other stone, until when the Book is finished
there rises before you this matchless temple of
God's truth, perfect in every outline and every
detail; not one stone too many and not one stone
too few, and yet every stone cut into its final
shape in the quarry from which it was taken.
How are you to account for it? There is but one
rational way to account for it, and that is, that
back of the human hands that wrought was the
master-mind of God that thought and gave to
each individual workman his specifications for
the work. You can't get around it and be honest
and fair.

THIRD TALK

I HAVE given you thus far three reasons why I believe the Bible to be the Word of God. First, because of the testimony of Jesus Christ to that effect. We saw that Jesus Christ set the stamp of His authority upon the entire Old Testament and the entire New Testament, and that if we accepted the authority of Jesus Christ we had to accept the entire Bible as of divine origin and authority. Then we saw that we must accept the authority of Jesus Christ, for He was accredited to us by five unmistakable divine testimonies. My second reason was because of its fulfilled prophecies. We saw that the Bible had the power of looking into the future and predicting with minuteness and exactness things which were to occur hundreds of years ahead, and that these prophecies were fulfilled to the letter, and that a Book which had this power of looking into the future and telling with minuteness, exactness, and precision things that were to come to pass must have for its author the only One in the universe who knows the end from the beginning—that is God. Our third reason for believing the Bible to be the Word of God was because of the unity of the Book. We saw that though the Bible was composed of sixty-six books, written by at least forty human authors, the period of their composition extending over at least 1500 years, and displaying every form of literary structure, that there was one all-pervading thought and purpose through the entire Book, that every part of the Book fitted into every other part, and that the Bible was the most thoroughly one Book of any book extant, and that the only way of accounting for this undeniable and remarkable phenomenon was that back of the many human authors was the one all-governing, all-controlling, all-superintending, all-shaping mind of God.

My fourth reason for believing the Bible to be the Word of God is because of the immeasurable superiority of its teachings to those of any other or all other books. It was quite the fashion when I was studying in theological halls to compare the teachings of the Bible with those of ethnic seers and philosophers, with the teachings of Socrates, Plato, Marcus Aurelius Antoninus, Epictetus, Isocrates, Seneca, Buddha, Zoroaster, Confucius, Mencius, and Mohammed. This is getting to be the fashion again. Anyone who institutes such a comparison and puts the Bible in the same class with these other teachers must be either ignorant of the teachings of the Bible or of the teachings of these ethnic seers and philosophers, or what is more frequently the case, ignorant of both. There are three points of radical difference between the teachings of the Bible and those of any other book.

First, these other teachers contain truth, but truth mixed with error. The Bible contains nothing but truth. There are gems of thought in these ethnic writers, but as Joseph Cook said years ago, " Jewels picked out of the mud." For example, we are often asked: " Did not Socrates teach most beautifully how a philosopher ought to die?" He did, but they forget to tell us that he also taught a woman of the town how to conduct her business that was not quite so nice. Again they ask us: "Did not Marcus Aurelius Antoninus teach most excellently about clemency?" He did. It is well worth reading; but they forget to tell us that he also taught that it was right to put people to death for no other crime than that of being Christians, and being himself Emperor of Rome, and, having power to do it, he practised what he preached. " Did not Seneca," they ask, "discourse finely about the advantages of poverty?" He did, but they forget to tell us that Seneca himself was at the time one of the worst spendthrifts in Rome, the onyx tables alone in his mansion costing a fabulous fortune. Moreover, he was the tutor under whose influence the most infamous emperor that Rome ever had, Nero, was brought up. " Did not Confucius," they ask again, " set forth ad-

mirably the duty of children to parents?" He
did, but they forget to tell us that Confucius also
taught that it was right to tell lies on occasion,
and unblushingly tells us that he himself practised lying on occasions. And there is perhaps
nothing in which his most devoted followers,
the Chinese, have followed so closely in the foot-
steps of their great master as in this matter of
lying. The Chinese have reduced lying to a fine
art, and a typical Chinaman will tell anything
" to save his face."

The second point of difference is that these
other writings contain part of the truth, while the
Bible contains all the truth. There is not a single known truth on moral or spiritual subjects
that cannot be found within the covers of the
Bible. This is a most remarkable fact—the
Bible is an old Book, and yet man in all his thinking before and since the Bible was written has
not discovered one single truth on moral or spiritual subjects that cannot be found in substance
within the covers of the Bible. In other words,
if all other books were destroyed and the Bible
left, we would suffer no essential loss on moral
and spiritual subjects, but if the Bible were destroyed and all other books left, the loss would
be irreparable. Why is this, if the Bible is men's
book as other books are men's books? Oftentimes I have challenged anyone in my audiences
to bring forward one single truth on moral or
spiritual subjects that I could not find within the

Bible,—it is quite conceivable that someone should succeed in doing this, for I do not pretend to know everything that is in the Bible; I have only been studying it a little over a quarter of a century,—but no one has been able to do it yet.

The third point of radical difference is this, that the Bible contains more truth than all other books put together. You can go to all literature, ancient and modern, the literature of ancient Greece, ancient Rome, ancient India, ancient Persia, and ancient China, and all modern literature as well, cull out of it all that is good, throw away all that is bad or worthless, bring together the result of your labor into one book, and even then you will not have a book that will take the place of this one Book. Why is it, if the Bible is men's book as other books are men's books, that in all the thousands of years of men's thinking, in all the millions of books that they have produced, men have not been able, all of them put together, to produce so much of real and priceless wisdom as is contained in this one Book? The answer is plain—other books are men's books, the Bible stands alone as God's Book.

My fifth reason for believing the Bible to be the Word of God is because of the history of the Book, its omnipotence against all men's attacks. What man has made, man can destroy. But eighteen centuries of most strenuous and determined assault have been unable to destroy or undermine intelligent faith in the Bible. Scarcely was the Bible given to the world before men discovered three things about it: First, that it condemned sin. Second, that it demanded renunciation of self. Third, that it laid human pride in the dust. Men were not willing to give up sin, not willing to renounce self, not willing to have their pride laid in the dust, therefore they hated the Book that made these demands. Man's hatred of the Bible has been most intense and most active. It determined on the destruction of the Book that it hated. Man after man has arisen with the determination to destroy this Book. Celsus tried it, with the brilliancy of his genius, and he failed. Then Porphyry tried it, with the depth of his philosophy, and he failed. Lucien tried it, with the keenness of his satire, and he failed. Then Diocletian came on the scene of action and tried other weapons; he brought to bear against the Bible all the military and political power of the strongest empire the world ever knew at the height of its glory. He issued edicts that every Bible should be burned, but that failed. Stronger edicts were issued— that those who owned Bibles should be put to death, and that failed. For eighteen centuries the attack upon the Bible has gone on. Every engine of destruction that human wisdom, human science, human philosophy, human wit, human satire, human force, and human brutality could bring to bear against a book have been brought to bear against this Book, and the Bible still stands. At times all the great of earth have been against it and only an obscure remnant for it, but still the Bible has more than held its own. It has to-day a firmer hold upon the confidence and affection of the best and wisest men and women than it ever had before in the world's history. If the Bible had been man's book, it would have gone down and been forgotten centuries ago; but because there is in this Book not only the hiding of God's wisdom, but the hiding of His power, it has wonderfully fulfilled the words of Jesus, "Heaven and earth shall pass away, but My words shall not pass away."

At times it has seemed to some, amid the deafening roar of the enemies' artillery and the dense smoke of battle, as if the Bible must have gone down; but when the smoke has rolled up from the field of conflict this impregnable citadel of God's eternal truth has reared its lofty head heavenward, unscathed, without one stone dislodged from foundation to highest parapet. Each new assault upon the Bible has simply served to illustrate anew the absolute omnipotence of this God-given Book. In a way, I rejoice in every new attack that is made upon the Bible. I tremble for certain weak-minded men and women who are willing to swallow anything that they are assured is the consensus of the latest scholarship; but for the Bible itself I have no fears. A Book that has successfully withstood eighteen centuries of assault of the devil's heaviest artil-

lery is not going down before the air-guns of
modern criticism.

Sixth. My sixth reason for believing the Bible
to be the Word of God is because of the influence
of the Book, its power to lift men up to God.
Every candid man must see and admit that there
is a power in this Book to brighten and gladden
and beautify and ennoble human lives, to lift
men up to God, that no other book possesses. A
stream can rise no higher than its source, and a
Book that has a power to lift men up to God
that no book possesses, must have come down
from God in a way no other book has. In literally millions of cases this Book has demonstrated
its power to reach down to men and women in
the deepest depths of iniquity and degradation
and lift them up, up, up, up, until they were fit
for a place beside the Christ upon the throne. I
recall a man of brilliant parts, but stupefied and
brutalized and demonized by drink, and this man
was an agnostic. I urged him to accept the
Bible and the Christ of the Bible, but with a
hollow laugh he said: " I don't believe in your
Bible or your Christ. I am an agnostic." But
at last, sunken to the lowest depths of ruin, he
threw his agnosticism to the winds and accepted
this Book and the Christ of this Book, and by
the power of this Book was transformed into one
of the truest, noblest, humblest men I know.
What other book could do it? This Book has
power, not only to lift individuals, but nations

Godwards. We owe all that is best in our modern civilization, in our political, commercial, and domestic life, to the influence of this Book. The man who attacks the Book is attacking the very foundations of all that is best in modern civilization. The man who attacks the Bible is the worst enemy that an individual or society has.

Seventh, I believe the Bible to be the Word of God, because of the character of those who accept it as such, and because of the character of those who reject it. Two things speak for the Divine origin of this Book—the character of those who are sure that it is the Word of God, and the character of those who deny it. Oftentimes when some man or woman says to me, " I believe firmly the Bible to be the Word of God," and when I look at the purity, the beauty, the humility, the devotion to God and man that there is in their character, how near they live to God, I feel like saying, " I am glad that you do believe the Bible to be the Word of God. The fact that one who lives so near God, and knows God as well as you do, believes the Bible to be His Book, is a confirmation of my own faith that it is." On the other hand, oftentimes when men with a self-confident toss of the head say, " I do not believe the Bible is the Word of God," and when I look at the sinfulness or selfishness or smallness or sordidness of their lives, how far they live from God, I feel like saying, " I am glad that you do not. The fact that a man who is living upon the plane that you are living, living so far from God, and knows God so little, doubts that the Bible is the Word of God, is a confirmation of my own faith that it is." Do not misunderstand me. I do not mean by this that every man who professes to believe in the Bible is better than every man who rejects the Bible; but what I do mean is this, show me a man who is living a life of absolute surrender to God, living under the control of the Spirit of God, living a life of devotion to the highest welfare of his fellowmen, a life of humility and of prayer, and I will show you every time a man who believes the Bible to be God's Word. On the other hand, show me a man who denies or persistently questions whether the Bible is the Word of God, and I will show you a man that is leading either (mind you, I say " either," not " all ") a life of greed for gold, or of lust, or of self-will, or of spiritual pride. I challenge any man to furnish me an exception. I have been looking for one literally around the world, and I have never found one. An attempt to furnish an exception has been made a number of times, but it is simply laughable to think of the men suggested as leading lives of " humility and prayer," or to think of them as not leading lives of " self-will." Anyone who has not surrendered absolutely to God is leading a life of " self-will." In other words, all who live nearest God and know God best are sure that the Bible is God's Word.

Those who have most doubts about it are those who are living farthest from God and know God least. Which will you believe? Suppose that there were discovered in the city of Boston a manuscript which purported to be by Oliver Wendell Holmes, but that there was great discussion among the critics as to whether or not Oliver Wendell Holmes were the real author. Finally it was submitted to a committee of critics for decision, and it was discovered that all those critics who knew Oliver Wendell Holmes best, who lived in most intimate fellowship with him, who were most in sympathy with his thought, were absolutely unanimous in their declaration that the manuscript was by him, and that those who questioned it were those who knew Oliver Wendell Holmes the least, and had the least fellowship with him, and were least in sympathy with his thought, which would you believe? That is a very simple question in literary criticism, much simpler than that which our modern critics so confidently undertake to solve, namely, as to who may be the seven different authors of a single verse in a book written thousands of years ago, as is attempted in that monumental joke book of the nineteenth century, the Polychrome Bible. Now this is the precise case with the Bible; all who live nearest God and know God best, all who are in most intimate fellowship with Him, are of absolutely one accord in saying that the Bible is His work. Those who have

the most doubts about it are those who live farthest from Him and know God least.

There is another significant fact, that the
nearer men get to God, the more confident they
become that the Bible is His Word. The far-
ther they drift from God, the more doubts enter
their hearts. The following is a case of con-
stant occurrence, that a man who is a sinner and
an unbeliever, by the mere fact of giving up his
sin without further argument is delivered from
his unbelief. Can anyone cite one single instance of an opposite kind, where one was a sinner and a believer, and by the fact of his giving
up his sin lost his faith?

Furthermore, how often does it occur that a
man, who at one period was living a life of con-
secration, of nearness to God, and enjoyed a
serene and undisturbed faith that the Bible was
God's Word, begins to prosper in the things of
this world, the love of money enters his heart,
he drifts away, from the out-and-out separation
of his life to God, and as he drifts from God he
drifts into doubt and into lax views about the
Bible. We see this to-day upon every hand—
men who are becoming lax in their morals also
becoming lax in their doctrine. Broad morals
and broad theology go hand in hand; they are
twin brothers. So true is this that oftentimes
when men tell me that they are getting into
doubt, I put to them the question, " What have
you been doing? " Once, walking in a univer-

sity town, I saw a little way ahead of me on the street a young fellow that I knew. I caught up with him and said to him, " Charlie, how are you getting on? " and with a self-satisfied look he said, " Well, to tell you the truth, Mr. Torrey, I am getting somewhat skeptical." I said, " Charlie, what have you been doing? " The poor fellow blushed and dropped his head. Charlie had been sinning, and sin had begotten doubt. This is the history of the genesis of doubt in the hearts of thousands of men to-day.

Where is the stronghold of the Bible? The pure, happy, unselfish home. Where is the stronghold of infidelity? The public-house, the race-course, the gambling hell, and the brothel. Suppose that I should come, a stranger to your city, and should go into one of your public-houses with a Bible under my arm, lay my Bible down upon the bar, and order a glass of whisky straight, and add, " Make it big," what would happen? There would be great surprise. Quite likely the bartender would say, " Pardon me, but what is that book? Is not that the Bible? " " Yes." " And what did you ask for—a tumbler of whisky straight? " " Yes, and make it large." He would not know what to make of it. But suppose I should enter the public-house and lay upon the bar a copy of any work of Ingersoll or of Bradlaugh, a copy of the *Clarion,* or the *Agnostic Journal,* or *Freethinker,* or the most respectable infidel book or paper that there is, and order a glass of whisky straight, I would get it without a question or a look of surprise. It would be just what they would expect. The Bible and whisky don't go together. Infidelity and whisky do go together. When I was in Belfast I made this remark, and at the close of the address a physician came to me laughing, and said: "We had yesterday an illustration of just what you said. After your afternoon Bible reading my mother went into a licensed grocer's to get a little brandy for a friend who was ill. She had her Bible in her hand, and, without thinking, was trying to put it into the bag that she carried. The clerk who was waiting upon her said: 'That is right, madam, hide it. The two don't go well together.'"

FOURTH TALK

IN the three previous addresses I have given you seven reasons why I believe the Bible to be the Word of God. First, because of the testimony of Jesus Christ to that effect. We saw that Jesus Christ set the stamp of His authority upon the entire Old Testament and the entire New Testament, and that if we accepted the authority of Jesus Christ we were obliged to accept the entire Bible as to divine origin and authority. We next saw that we must accept the authority of Jesus Christ, for He was accredited to us by five unmistakably definite testimonies. First, by the testimony of the divine life that He lived; second, by the testimony of the divine words that He spoke; third, by the testimony of the divine works that He wrought; fourth, by the testimony of His divine influence upon all subsequent history; and fifth, by the testimony of the resurrection from the dead, which was God's divine attestation to the claims of Jesus Christ. The second reason I gave was because of its fulfilled prophecies. We saw that the Bible had the

43

power of looking into the future, and predicting with minuteness, accuracy, and precision things which were to occur hundreds of years ahead, and that these prophecies had been fulfilled to the letter. We concluded that a book which had this power of looking into the future and telling with minuteness, accuracy, and precision things that were to come to pass centuries afterwards must have for its Author the only One in the universe who knows the end from the beginning— that is, God. The third reason I gave for believing the Bible to be the Word of God was because of the unity of the Book. We saw that though the Bible was composed of sixty-six books, written by at least forty human authors, the period of their composition extending over at least 1500 years, and displaying every form of literary structure, that there was one all-pervading thought and purpose through the entire Book, that every part of the Bible fitted into every other part, and that the Bible was the most thoroughly one Book of any book extant. We saw that the only way to account for this undeniable and remarkable phenomenon was that back of the human authors was the one all-governing, all-controlling, all-superintending, all-shaping mind of God. The fourth reason for believing the Bible to be the Word of God was because of the immeasurable superiority of its teachings to those of any other book, or all other books. We saw that there were three points of radical difference

between the Bible and all other books: (1) That
other books contain truth, but truth mixed with
error, but the Bible contained nothing but truth;
(2) that other books contained part of the truth,
but the Bible contained all the truth; (3) that
the Bible contained more truth than all other
books together. The fifth reason was because of
the history of the Book, its omnipotence against
all men's attacks. We saw that what man had
produced man could destroy; but that eighteen
centuries of assault upon the Bible had utterly
failed to destroy the Book, or to undermine confidence in it. Our sixth reason for believing the
Bible to be the Word of God was because of its
power to lift men up to God. We saw that the
Bible has a power to lift men up to God that no
other book possesses, and must therefore have
come down from God in a way no other book has.
Our seventh reason for believing the Bible to be
the Word of God was because of the character
of those who accepted it as such and those who
rejected it. We saw that with absolute unanim-
ity all the men and women who lived nearest
God, and knew God best, believed the Bible to be
His Word, and that those who had the most
doubts about it were those who lived farthest
from God and knew God least.

My eighth reason for believing the Bible to be
the Word of God is because of the inexhaustible
depth of the Book. What man has produced
man can exhaust. But eighteen centuries of

study on the part of tens of thousands of the
ablest minds have been unable to exhaust the
Bible. Many men of strongest intellect, of marvellous powers of penetration, of broadest culture, have given a lifetime to the study of the
Bible, and no man who has really studied it has
ever dreamed of saying that he had gotten to the
bottom of the Book. Indeed, the more profoundly one digs into the Book, the more clearly
he sees that there are still unfathomable depths
of wisdom beneath him in this inexhaustible mine
of truth. Not only is this true of individuals,
it is true also of generations of men. Thousands
of men in co-operation with one another have
delved into this mine, but, so far from exhaust-
ing it, there are still new treasures of truth
awaiting each new student of the Word. New
light is constantly breaking forth from the Word
of God. How are we to account for this unquestionable fact? The human mind has been
progressing during these eighteen centuries—we
have outgrown every other book that belongs to
the past, but so far from outgrowing the Bible
we have not yet grown up to it. The Bible is
not only up to date, but always ahead of date.
The best interpretation of the most recent events
of our own day is found in this old Book. If
this Book were man's book we would have fath-
omed it centuries ago, but the fact that it has
proved itself unfathomable for eighteen centuries is positive proof that in it are hidden the

infinite treasures of the wisdom and knowledge
of God. A brilliant Unitarian writer in America has given utterance to one of the keenest
sentences that was ever spoken or written from
the standpoint of the denial of the inspiration of
the Bible. He says: "How irreligious to accuse
an infinite God with having put His whole wisdom in one so small a Book!" I submit that
that is keen, but this writer did not see how the
keen edge of his Damascus blade could be turned
against himself. What a testimony to the divine origin of this Book that such infinite wisdom can be packed in so small a compass! The
Bible is not such a very large Book (I have a
copy that I carry in my vest pocket), but yet in
a Book that can be printed in so small a compass there are packed away such treasures of
wisdom that eighteen centuries of study by the
world's best minds have been unable to exhaust
it. How are we to account for it? There is no
one but God who could pack such infinite treasures of truth in so small a compass.

My ninth reason for believing the Bible to be
the Word of God is because of the fact that as I
grow in knowledge and in character, in wisdom
and in holiness, I grow toward the Bible. The
nearer I get to God the nearer I get to the Bible.
When I began the real study of the Bible I had
the same experience with it that every thoughtful student has had in the beginning of his studies. I found things in the Bible that were diffi-

cult to understand, others that seemed incredible.
I found that the teachings of one part of the
Book seemed to flatly contradict the teachings of
other parts of the Book. It seemed clear to me
that if one teaching of the Bible were true, that
some other could not be, and like so many
another, I accepted so much of the Bible as was
wise enough to agree with me. But as I went
on studying the Bible, and as I went on growing
in likeness to God, I found that my difficulties
were disappearing; at first, one by one, then by
twos, and then by scores, ever disappearing more
and more. I found constantly that the nearer I
got to God, the nearer I got to the Bible; then
nearer still to God meant nearer still to the
Bible; and nearer yet to God meant nearer yet
to the Bible. What is the inevitable mathemati-
cal conclusion? Two lines always converging
as they draw near to a given point must meet
when they reach that point. The nearer I got
to God, the nearer I got to the Bible; the nearer
I got to God, the nearer I got to the Bible; the
nearer I got to God, the nearer I got to the Bible.
When I and God meet, I and the Bible will meet.
That is, the Bible was written from God's standpoint. There is no honest escaping of this
conclusion.

Suppose I were to pass through a vast, dark,
and dangerous forest for the first time. Before
starting upon this perilous tour a guide was
brought to me who had often been through the

forest before, and had conducted many a party through in safety, and had never led a single party astray. Under his leadership I began my journey through the forest. We got on very nicely together for a ways, but after a time we came to a place where two roads diverged. The guide said to me: "The path to the right is the right path to take." But my judgment and reason passing upon the phenomena observable by the senses saw clear indication that the road to the left was the road to take. I say to the guide: "I know that you have been through this forest time and again; that you have conducted many a party through in safety, and I have great confidence in your judgment upon that account, but in the present instance I believe you are wrong. My reason and judgment passing upon the phenomena that I can observe by my senses see clear indications that the road to the left is the road to take. Now I have never been through this forest before, and you have, and I know that my reason and judgment are not infallible, but they are the best guide that I have, and I cannot throw them overboard. I must follow them." So I take the road to the left. I go about a mile and then come to an impassable morass, and have to go back and take the way the guide said. We get on well together again for a ways, but again we come to a place where two paths diverge. This time the guide says: "The road to the left is the road to take." But my reason and judgment passing upon the phenomena observable by my senses see clear indication that the road to the right is the road to take, and again we have our little parley. Again I say to the guide: " I know that you have passed through this forest time and again, and that you never led a party astray, and I have great confidence in your judgment on that account, but my reason and common sense passing upon the phenomena observable by my senses tell me that the road to the right is the road to take. Now, I know that my reason and common sense are not infallible, but they are the best guide that I have, and I cannot throw them overboard." So again I go the way my reason and common sense passing upon the phenomena observable by my senses suggest. I go about half a mile, and then run up against an impassable barrier of rock, and have to go back and go the way the guide said. Suppose that this should happen fifty times, and every time the guide proved right, and my reason and common sense, passing upon the phenomena observable by the senses, proved wrong, do you not think that about the fifty-first time I would have reason and common sense enough to throw my ever-erring judgment to the winds and go the way the guide said? This has been my exact experience with the Bible. Time and time again I have come to the parting of the ways, where the Bible said one thing and my reason and common sense seemed to say another, and, fool that I was,

I threw the Bible overboard and went the way that my reason and common sense said, and every time I have had to come back and go the way the Bible said. I trust that the next time when I and the Bible differ I will have common sense enough to throw my ever-erring reason and judgment overboard and go the way the Bible says. The most irrational thing in the world is what we call rationalism. Rationalism is an attempt to subject the teachings of infinite wisdom to the criticism of our finite judgment. Could anything possibly be more irrational than that? It never seems to occur to the rationalist that God can have a good reason for saying or doing a thing if he, the rationalist, cannot see the reason. One of the greatest discoveries that I ever made was one day when it dawned upon me that God might possibly know more than I did, and that God might possibly be right, when to me He appeared to be wrong.

My tenth reason for believing the Bible to be the Word of God is because of the testimony of the Holy Spirit to that fact. To the one who puts himself in the right attitude toward God and truth, the Holy Spirit bears direct testimony that the voice that speaks to him from the Bible is the voice of God. One will often meet a godly old woman, of no very wide reading or culture, who still has a firm faith that the Bible is the Word of God. If you ask her why she believes the Bible to be the Word of God, she will reply:

" I *know* the Bible to be the Word of God." But
again if you ask, " *Why* do you believe it to be
the Word of God?" she will reply: " I *know* it to
be the Word of God." And if still again you
ask: " *Why* do you believe it to be the Word of
God?" again she will reply: " I *know* it to be
the Word of God." Very likely you will say:
" Well, I will not disturb the old lady's faith "
(no fear, you couldn't if you would), " but she is
beneath argument." You are mistaken, she is
above argument. Jesus Christ says: " He that
is of God heareth God's words " (John viii. 47).
Again Jesus Christ says: " My sheep hear my
voice " (John x. 27). She is one of God's children, and knows her Father's voice, and she
knows that the voice that speaks to her from the
Bible is the voice of God. She is one of Christ's
sheep, and she knows that the voice that speaks
to her from the Bible is the voice of the true
Shepherd.

I can tell you how anyone of you can come to
that same position, where you will be able to distinguish God's voice, and to know that the voice
that speaks to you from the Bible is the voice of
God. Jesus Christ Himself tells us this in John
vii. 17, R.V.: " If any man willeth to do His will,
he shall know of the teaching whether it be of
God, or whether I speak from myself." The
surrender of the will to God opens the eyes of
the soul to see the truth of God. Jesus Christ
does not demand that a man shall believe with-

out evidence, but He does demand that a man shall put himself in that moral attitude toward God and the truth that makes him competent to appreciate evidence. There is nothing that so clarifies the human mind as the surrender of the will to God. Some years ago I was lecturing to our students in Chicago on how to deal with skeptics and infidels. Our lecture room in Chicago is open to all kinds and conditions of men, and oftentimes it is a motley crowd that gathers together—Christian and Jew, Roman Catholic and Protestant, believers, skeptics, infidels, agnostics, and atheists. At the close of this lecture the wife of the late Dr. A. J. Gordon of Boston came to me and said: "Did you see the man sitting near me as you spoke?" I had noticed the man, because I had had some little conversation with him before. "Well," she added, "while you were speaking I heard him say, 'I wish he would try it upon me.'" "I would be glad to." "Well, there he is over in the corner." I did not need to go to him, for when the others had gone out he came to me and said: "Mr. Torrey, I do not wish to say anything discourteous, but really my experience contradicts everything that you have said to these students this morning." I replied: "Have you done what I told these students to get the infidel or skeptic to do, and guaranteed if they would do it they would come out of their doubt and unbelief into a clear faith in the Bible as the Word of God

and Jesus as the Son of God?" "Yes, I have
done it all." "Now," I said, "let's be definite
about this." So I called my secretary and dictated something like this: "I believe that there
is an absolute difference between right and
wrong" (I did not say, I believe that there is a
God, for this man was an agnostic, and neither
affirmed nor denied the existence of God, and
you have to begin where a man is), "and I
hereby take my stand upon the right to follow it
wherever it carries me. I promise to make an
honest search to find if Jesus Christ is the Son
of God, and if I find that He is, I promise to accept Him as my Saviour, and confess Him publicly before the world." My secretary brought
two copies of this, and I handed them to him and
said: "Are you willing to sign this?" He replied: "Certainly," and signed them both. He
folded one and put it in his pocket. I folded the
other and put it in my pocket. Then he added:
"There is nothing in it. My case is very peculiar." (His case was peculiar. He had been
through Unitarianism, Spiritualism, Theosophy,
and pretty much all other isms, and was now an
out-and-out agnostic.) "Another thing," I
added, "do you know that there is not a God?"
"No," he said, "I don't know that there is not a
God. Any man is a fool to say he knows that
there is not a God. I am an agnostic; I neither
affirm nor deny." I said: "Well, I know that
there is a God, but that won't do you any good.

Do you know that God does not answer prayer?"
" No, I do not know that God does not answer
prayer. I do not believe that He answers prayer,
but I do not know that He does not answer
prayer." "Well," I said, " I know that He does
answer prayer, but that will not do you any good;
but here is a possible clue to knowledge. You
are a graduate of a British University?" "Yes."
" You know the method of modern science?
The method of modern science is this, if one
finds a possible clue to knowledge, to follow that
possible clue to see what there may be in it.
Here is a possible clue. Will you adopt the
methods of modern science in religious investi-
gation? Will you follow out this possible clue
to see what there may be in it? Will you offer
this prayer, ' Oh, God, if there be any God, show
me if Jesus Christ is Thy Son or not, and if Thou
showest me that He is Thy Son, I promise to
accept Him as my Saviour, and confess Him as
such before the world?'" "Yes," he said, " I
will do that, too; but there is nothing in it. My
case is very peculiar." "One more thing," I
said. "John says in John xx. 31: ' These are
written that ye might believe that Jesus is the
Christ, the Son of God, and that believing ye
might have life through His name.' Now John
tells us here that the Gospel of John is written
to show men the proof that Jesus is the Christ,
the Son of God. Will you read the proof? Will
you read the Gospel of John?" "I have read

it again and again," he replied; "I can quote parts of it to you if you wish to hear them." " No," I said, " but I wish you to read it this time in a new way. Each time before you read offer this prayer, ' Oh, God, if there be any God, show me what of truth there is in the verses I am about to read, and what you show me to be true, I promise to accept and take my stand upon.' Now don't read too many verses at a time. Don't try to believe or disbelieve. Simply be open to conviction to the truth; pay careful attention to what you read; and when you have finished the Gospel report to me the result." " Yes," he said, " I will do it all; but there is nothing in it. My case is very peculiar." " Never mind," I said, and went over again the three things he had promised to do, and we separated. About two weeks after I was speaking on the South Side, and I saw this man in the hall. At the close of the meeting he came to me and said: " There was something in that." I replied: " I knew that before." " Well," he said, " ever since I have done what I promised I would do, it is just as if I had been caught up and was being carried along by the Niagara River, and the first thing I know I shall be a shouting Methodist." I became a Methodist for the occasion, and said: " Praise the Lord! " I went East to lecture at some schools in Massachusetts. When I came back there was a reception, and this man was present at the reception, and he came to me and said: "Are you busy?" "Not too busy to speak to you," I replied. We went into another room, and he said: "I cannot understand it. I cannot see how I ever listened to these men" (mentioning a number of infidel and Unitarian writers and speakers). "It is all nonsense to me now." "Oh," I said, "the Bible explains that in I Cor. ii. 14: 'The natural man receiveth not the things of the Spirit of God: for they are foolishness unto him: neither can he know them, because they are spiritually discerned.' You have taken the right attitude towards truth, and God has opened your eyes to see the truth." He came out into a clear faith in Jesus Christ as the Son of God, and the Bible as the Word of God. If any of you doubt this story, try it for yourself, and you will have one of your own to tell.

Gentlemen, the Bible is the Word of God. The voice that speaks to us from this Book is the voice of God. But someone will say: "Suppose it's the Word, what of it?" Everything of it! If the Bible be the Word of God, then Jesus Christ is the Son of God, and there is no salvation for any of us outside of a living faith in Him that leads us to put all our trust for pardon in His atoning work on the cross of Calvary, and to surrender our wills and our lives absolutely to His control. Have you done this? Will you do it now?

FIFTH TALK

THE resurrection of Jesus Christ is in many respects the most important fact in history. It is the Gibraltar of Christian evidences, the Waterloo of infidelity. If it can be proven to be a historic certainty that Jesus rose from the dead, then Christianity rests upon an impregnable foundation. Every essential truth of Christianity is involved in the resurrection. If the resurrection stands, every essential doctrine of Christianity stands. If the resurrection goes down, every essential doctrine of Christianity goes down. Intelligent skeptics and infidels realize this. A leading skeptic has recently said that there is no use wasting time discussing the other miracles; the essential question is, Did Jesus Christ rise from the Dead? If He did, it is easy enough to believe the other miracles. If He did not, the other miracles must go. I am confident that this skeptic has correctly stated the case.

There are three separate lines of proof of the truthfulness of the statements contained in the four Gospels regarding the resurrection of Jesus Christ.

First, *the external evidence for the authenticity and truthfulness of the Gospel narratives.* This is an altogether satisfactory argument, but we shall not enter into it at this time. The argument is long and intricate, and it would take many days to discuss it satisfactorily. The other arguments are so completely sufficient that we can do without this, good as it is in its place.

Second, the second argument is based upon *the internal proofs of the truthfulness of the Gospel records.* This argument is thoroughly conclusive, and we shall proceed to state it briefly. We shall not assume anything whatever. We shall not assume that the four Gospel records are true history. We shall not assume that the four Gospels were written by the men whose names they bear. We shall not even assume that they were written in the century in which Jesus is alleged to have lived, died, and risen again, nor in the next century, nor in the next. We will assume nothing whatever. We will start out with a fact which we all know to be true, namely, that we have the four Gospels today, whoever wrote them. We shall place the four Gospels side by side and see if we can discern in them the marks of truth or of fiction.

The first thing we notice as we compare these Gospels one with the other is that *they are four separate and independent accounts.* This appears plainly from the apparent discrepancies in the four different accounts. These apparent dis-

crepancies are marked and many. It would
have been impossible for four accounts to have
been made up in collusion with one another and
so many and so marked discrepancies be found
in them. There is a harmony between the four
accounts, but the harmony does not lie upon the
surface, but only comes out by protracted and
thorough study. It is just such a harmony as
would exist between accounts written by several
different persons, each looking at the events
recorded from his own standpoint. It is just such
a harmony as would not exist in four accounts
manufactured in collusion. In four accounts
manufactured in collusion, whatever of harmony there was would have appeared on the
surface, whatever discrepancy there was would
only have come out by minute and careful study;
but the case is just the opposite. The fact is,
that the harmony comes out by minute and careful study; the apparent discrepancy lies upon the
surface. Whether true or false, these four accounts are separate and independent from one
another. The four accounts supplement one
another, a third account sometimes reconciling
apparent discrepancies of two.

It is plain that these accounts must be either a
record of facts that actually occurred, or else
fictions. If fictions, they must have been fabricated in one of two ways, either independently of
one another, or in collusion with one another.
They cannot have been made up independently;

the agreements are too marked and too many. They cannot have been made up in collusion; as already seen, the apparent discrepancies are too numerous and too noticeable. Not made up independently, not made up in collusion, therefore it is evident that they were not made up at all. They are a true relation of facts as they actually occurred.

The next thing that we notice is that these accounts *bear striking indications of having been derived from eye-witnesses.* The account of an eye-witness is readily distinguishable from that of one who is merely retailing what others have told him. Anyone who is accustomed to weigh evidence in court, or in historical study, soon learns how to distinguish the account of an eye-witness from mere hearsay evidence. Any careful student of the Gospel records of the resurrection will readily detect many marks of an eye-witness. Some years ago, when lecturing at an American University, a gentleman was introduced to me as being a skeptic. I asked him what course of study he was pursuing. He replied that he was pursuing a post-graduate course in history with a view to an historical professorship. I said: " Then you know that the account of an eye-witness differs in marked respects from the account of one who is simply telling what he has heard from others?" He replied: "Yes." I then asked: "Have you carefully read the four Gospel accounts of the resurrec-

tion of Christ?" He answered: "I have."
"Tell me, hav· you not noticed clear indications
that they were .erived from eye-witnesses?"
"Yes," he replied, "I have been greatly struck
by this in reading the accounts." Anyone else
who carefully and intelligently reads them will
be struck by the same fact.

The third thing that we notice about these
Gospel narratives is *their naturalness, straightforwardness, artlessness, and simplicity.* The
accounts indeed have to do with the supernatural,
but the accounts themselves are most natural.
There is an absolute absence of all attempt
at coloring and effect. The simple, straightforward telling of facts as they occurred. It
sometimes happens that when a witness is on
the witness stand that the story he tells is so artless, so straightforward, so natural, there is such
an entire absence of any attempt at coloring
and effect, that his testimony bears weight independently of anything we may know of the character or previous history of the witness. As we
listen to his story we say to ourselves: "This
man is telling the truth." The weight of this
kind of evidence is greatly increased, and reaches
practical certainty, when we have several independent witnesses of this sort, all bearing testimony to the same essential facts, but with va-
rieties of detail, one omitting what another tells,
and the third unconsciously reconciling apparent
discrepancies between the two. This is the pre·

cise case with the four Gospel narratives of the resurrection of Christ. The Gospel authors do not seem to have reflected at all upon the meaning or bearing of many of the facts which they relate. They simply tell right out what they saw, in all simplicity and straightforwardness, leaving the philosophizing to others. Dr. William Furness, the great Unitarian scholar and critic, who certainly was not overmuch disposed in favor of the supernatural, says: " Nothing can exceed in artlessness and simplicity the four acounts of the first appearance of Jesus after His crucifixion. If these qualities are not discernible here, we must despair of ever being able to discern them anywhere."

Suppose we should find four accounts of the battle of Monmouth. Nothing decisive was known as to the authorship of these accounts, but when we laid them side by side we found that they were manifestly independent accounts. We found, furthermore, striking indications that they were from eye-witnesses. We found them all marked by that artlessness, simplicity, and straightforwardness that carry conviction; we found that, while apparently disagreeing in minor details, they agreed substantially in their account of the battle—even though we had no knowledge of the authorship or date of these accounts, would we not in the absence of any other account say: " Here is a true account of the battle of Monmouth?" Now this is exactly the

case with the four Gospel narratives; manifestly
separate and independent from one another,
bearing the clear marks of having been derived
from eye-witnesses, characterized by an unri-
valled artlessness, simplicity, and straightforwardness, apparently disagreeing in minor details, but in perfect agreement as to the great
essential facts related, if we are fair and honest,
are we not logically driven to say: " Here is a
true account of the resurrection of Jesus?"

The next thing that we notice is *the unintentional evidence of words, phrases, and accidental
details.* It oftentimes happens that when a witness is on the stand the unintentional evidence
that he bears by words and phrases which he
uses, and by accidental details which he introduces, is more convincing than his direct testimony, because it is not the testimony of the witness, but the testimony of the truth to itself.
The Gospel stories abound in evidence of this
sort.

Take as a first instance the fact that, in all
the Gospel records of the resurrection, we are
given to understand that Jesus was not at first
recognized by His disciples when He appeared to
them after His resurrection (*e.g.,* Luke xxiv. 16;
John xxi. 4). We are not told why this is so, but
if we will think a while over it we can soon discover why it is so. But the Gospel narratives
simply record the fact without attempting to
explain it. If the stories were fictitious, they

would never have been made up in this way; for
the writers would have seen at once the objection that would have arisen in the minds of
those who did not wish to believe in the resurrection; that is, that it was not really Jesus whom
the disciples saw. Why then is the story told in
this way? For the very evident reason that the
evangelists were not making the story up for
effect, but recording events precisely as they occurred. This was the way it occurred, and
therefore this is the way in which they told it.
It is not a fabrication of imaginary incidents,
but an exact record of facts accurately observed
and accurately recorded.

Take a second instance. In all the Gospel
records of the appearances of Jesus after His
resurrection there is not a single recorded appearance to an enemy or opponent of Christ; all
the appearances were to those who were already
believers. Why this was so, we can easily see
by a little thought, but nowhere in the Gospels
are we told why it was so. If the stories were
made up, they certainly would never have been
made up in this way. If the Gospels are, as
some would have us believe, fabrications con-
structed 100, or 200, or 300 years after the alleged events recorded, when all the actors were
dead and gone, Jesus would have been represented as appearing to Caiaphas and Annas, and
Pilate and Herod, and confounding them by his
reappearance from the dead; but there is no sug-

gestion of anything of this kind in the Gospel
stories. Every appearance is to one who is already a believer. Why is this so? For the very
evident reason that this was the way that things
occurred, and the Gospel narratives are not concerned with producing a story for effect, but
simply with recording events precisely as they
occurred and as they were observed.

We find still another instance in the fact that
the recorded appearances of Jesus after His resurrection were only occasional. He would appear in the midst of His disciples and disappear,
and not be seen again perhaps for several days.
Why this was so we can easily discern. Jesus
was seeking to wean His disciples from their old-
time communion with Him in the body, and to
prepare them for the communion in the Spirit of
the days that were to come. We are not, how-
ever, told this in the Gospel narrative; we are
left to discover it for ourselves. It is doubtful
if the disciples themselves at the time realized
the meaning of the facts. If they had been
making up a story to produce effect, they would
have represented Jesus as being with them constantly, as living with them, eating and drinking
with them day after day. Why then is the story
told as recorded in the four Gospels? Because
this is the way that it had all occurred, and the
Gospel writers are simply concerned with giving
an exact representation of the facts as witnessed
by themselves and by others.

We find another very striking instance in what is recorded concerning the words of Jesus to Mary at their first meeting, in John xx. 17. Jesus is recorded as saying to Mary, " Touch me not, for I am not yet ascended to My Father." We are not told why Jesus said this to Mary. We are left to discover the reason for ourselves, if we can. The commentators have had a great deal of trouble discovering it. They vary widely from one another in their explanations of the words of Jesus. Go to the commentaries and you will find that one commentary gives one reason, and another another, and another another. I have a reason of my own that I have never seen in any commentary, but which I am persuaded is the true reason; but I have never been able to persuade others that it was the true reason. Why then is this little utterance of Jesus put in the Gospel record without a word of explanation, and which it has taken eighteen centuries to explain, and which is not altogether satisfactorily explained yet? Certainly a writer making up a story would not put in it a little detail without apparent meaning and without any attempt at an explanation of it. Stories that are made up are made up for a purpose; details that are inserted are inserted for a purpose, a purpose more or less evident; but eighteen centuries of study have not been able to find out the purpose why this is inserted. Why, then, is it there? Because this is exactly what happened. This

is what Jesus said; this is what Mary heard; this
is what Mary told; and therefore this is what
John recorded. We have here not a fiction, but
an accurate record of words spoken by Jesus
after His resurrection.

Another incidental detail that is introduced
in the Gospel narrative, and which is decisive
proof of its historical accuracy, is found in John
xix. 34. We are told that when one of the sol-
diers pierced the side of our crucified Lord with
a spear, that straightway there came out blood
and water. The reason of this we are not told.
In fact, the writer could not have known the
reason. There was no man on earth at the time
who had sufficient knowledge of physiology to
have told the reason. It was only centuries afterwards that the physiological reason was discovered. The distinguished medical authority,
Dr. Simpson, of Edinburgh University, the dis-
coverer of chloroform, wrote during his lifetime
an able brochure, in which he showed on scientific grounds that Jesus Christ died from what
is called in scientific language " extravasation
of the blood," or, in popular language, " a
broken heart." When one dies in this way the
arms are thrown out (of course Jesus' arms
were already stretched out on the Cross), there
is a loud cry (such as Jesus uttered, " My God,
My God, why hast Thou forsaken Me? "), the
blood escapes from the pericardium and prevents
the heart from beating. Then the blood stands

for a short time, it separates into serum (the water) and clot (the red corpuscles, blood). When the soldier pierced the bag (pericardium) the blood and water flowed out. This is the scientific explanation of the recorded fact, but John did not know this explanation. No one then living knew it, no one knew it for centuries afterwards. Is it conceivable that a writer in fabricating an account of events that never occurred should have made up and inserted a fact that has a strict scientific explanation, fitting precisely into the various facts recorded, but an explanation which neither he nor anyone living at the time could possibly have known? How, then, does it come to be recorded in this way? Because this is precisely what occurred, and though John did not know the explanation, he observed the fact, and recorded the fact as observed, and left it for time and scientific discovery to conclusively demonstrate the historical accuracy of what he told. Beyond a peradventure we have here no fiction, but an exact record of something that occurred and was observed precisely as recorded. In my next address I will give you many more and more striking illustrations of the self-evident and indubitable truthfulness of the Gospel accounts of the resurrection of Christ.

SIXTH TALK

In our address of yesterday we began the consideration of the question, "Did Jesus really rise from the dead?" We started out without assuming anything whatever; we did not assume that the four Gospels were true; we did not assume that the four Gospels were written by the men whose names they bear; we did not even assume that they were written in the century in which the events recorded were alleged to have occurred, nor the next century, nor the next. We started with the well-known fact that we have the four Gospels. Whether true or false, and whoever may have written them, we certainly have them. We laid these four Gospels side by side and tried to discover from the study of them whether they were the record of events that actually occurred or whether they were fiction. The first thing that we discovered was that they were separate and independent accounts. We saw that they must either be a true record of facts or else fiction; that if fiction they must have been fabricated in one of two ways, either independently of one another, or else in collusion with one another. We saw that they could not have been fabricated in collusion, the apparent discrepancies were too numerous and too noticeable; we saw that they could not have been made up independently, the agreements were too marked and too many. Not made up in collusion, not made up independently, then not made up at all—that is, they contain a true relation of facts as they actually occurred. We saw, in the next place, that each of the Gospel accounts bore striking indications of having been derived from eye-witnesses. We noted, in the third place, their artlessness, straightforwardness, and simplicity. We saw that it often happens that when a witness is on the stand, the story he tells is so artless, straightforward, simple, and natural that it carries conviction regardless of any knowledge we may have of the witness or of his previous character. We saw that each one of the Gospel stories had these characteristics which were clear proof of the truthfulness of the stories recorded. We noticed, in the next place, the unintentional evidence of words, phrases, and accidental details. We saw that it often happens that when an eye-witness is on the stand that the unintentional evidence he bears by words, phrases, and accidental details is more effective than his direct testimony, because it is not the testimony of the witness, but the testimony of the truth to itself. We

gave a number of illustrations of this; we are
to give still more to-day.

Turn to John xx. 24, 25, " But Thomas, one
of the twelve, called Didymus, was not with
them when Jesus came. The other disciples
therefore said unto him, We have seen the Lord.
But he said unto them, Except I shall see in His
hands the print of the nails, and put my finger
into the print of the nails, and thrust my hand
into His side, I will not believe." How true
this all is to life. It is in perfect harmony with
what is told us of Thomas elsewhere. Thomas
was the chronic doubter in the apostolic company, the man who always looked upon the dark
side, the man who was governed by the testimony
of his senses. It was he who, when Jesus said
in John xi. 15 that he was going again into
Judea, despondently said, " Let us also go that
we may die with Him." It was he again who,
in John xiv. 4, 5, when Jesus said, " Whither I
go ye know the way," replied, " Lord, we know
not whither Thou goest, and how can we know
the way?" And it is he that now says, " Except I shall see in His hands the print of the
nails, and put my finger into the print of the
nails, and thrust my hand into His side, I will
not believe." Is this made up, or is it life? To
make it up would require a literary art that im-
immeasurably exceeded the possibilities of the
author.

Turn again to John xx. 4-6: " So they ran

both together: and the other disciple did outrun Peter, and came first to the sepulcher. And he, stooping down and looking in, saw the linen clothes lying; yet went he not in. Then cometh Simon Peter following him, and went into the sepulcher." This is again in striking keeping with what we know of the men. Mary, returning hurriedly from the tomb, bursts in upon the two disciples, and cries, " They have taken away the Lord out of the sepulcher, and we know not where they have laid Him." John and Peter spring to their feet, and run at the top of their speed for the tomb. John was the younger of the two disciples. We are not told this in the narrative, but we learn it from other sources. Being younger, he was fleeter of foot and outran Peter, and reached the tomb first; but, man of retiring and reverent disposition, he did not enter the tomb, but simply stooped down and looked in. But impetuous older Peter comes lumbering along behind as fast as he can, but when once he reaches the tomb he never waits a moment outside, but plunges headlong in. Is this made up, or is it life? He was indeed a literary artist of consummate ability who had the skill to make this up if it did not happen just so. There is also incidentally a touch of local accuracy in the report. When one visits to-day the tomb which scholars now accept as the real burial place of Christ, he will find himself unconsciously obliged to *stoop down* to look in.

Turn again to John xxi. 7: "Therefore that
disciple whom Jesus loved saith unto Peter, It
is the Lord.   Now when Simon Peter heard that
it was the Lord, he girt his fisher's coat unto
him (for he was naked), and did cast himself
into the sea."   Here again we have the unmistakable marks of truth and life.   Recall the circumstances.   The apostles have gone at Jesus'
commandment into Galilee to meet Him there.
Jesus does not at once appear.   Simon Peter,
with the fisherman's passion still strong in his
bosom, says, "I go a-fishing!"   The others say,
"We also go with thee."   They fished all night
and caught nothing.   In the early dawn Jesus
stands upon the shore, but the disciples do not
recognize Him in the dim light.   Jesus says to
them, "Children, have ye aught to eat?"   And
they answer, "No."   He bids them cast the net
on the right side of the boat and they will find.
When the cast was made, they are not able to
draw it for the multitude of fishes.   In an instant
John, the man of quick, spiritual perception,
says, "It is the Lord."   No sooner does Peter,
the man of impulsive action, hear this, than he
grips his fisher's coat and throws it about his
naked form, and throws himself overboard and
strikes out for shore to reach his Lord.   Is this
made up, or is it life?   This is no fiction.   If
some unknown author of the fourth Gospel made
this up, he is the master literary artist of the
ages, and we should take down every other name

from the literary pantheon and place his above them all.

Take another illustration, John xx. 15: "Jesus saith unto her, Woman, why weepest thou? whom seekest thou? She, supposing Him to be the gardener, saith unto Him, Sir, if thou have borne Him hence, tell me where thou hast laid Him, and I will take Him away." Here is surely a touch that surpasses the art of any man of that day, or any day. Mary had gone into the city and notified Peter and John that she had found the sepulcher empty. They start on a run for the sepulcher. As Mary has already made the journey twice, they easily far outstrip her; but wearily and slowly she makes her way back to the tomb. Peter and John have been long gone when she reaches it. Broken-hearted, thinking that the tomb of her beloved Lord has been desecrated, she stands without, weeping. There are two angels sitting in the tomb, one at the head and the other at the foot where the body of Jesus had lain, but the grief-stricken woman has no eye for angels. They say unto her, "Woman, why weepest thou?" She replies, "Because they have taken away my Lord, and I know not where they have laid Him." A footfall is heard in the leaves at her back, and she turns herself about to see who is coming. She sees Jesus standing there, but, blinded by tears and despair, she does not recognize her Lord. Jesus says unto her, "Why weepest

thou? Whom seekest thou?" She supposes it
is the gardener who is talking to her, and says,
"Sir, if thou have borne Him hence, tell me
where thou hast laid Him, and I will take Him
away." Now remember who it is that makes
the offer, and what she offers to do; a weak
woman offers to carry away a full-grown man.
Of course she could not do it, but how true to
a woman's love that always forgets its weakness
and never stops at impossibilities. There is
something to be done, and she says, "I will do
it." "Tell me where thou hast laid Him, and
I will take Him away." Is this made up?
Never! This is life! This is reality! This is
truth!

Take still another illustration, Mark xvi. 7:
"But go your way, tell His disciples and Peter
that He goeth before you into Galilee: there
shall ye see Him, as He said unto you." "But
go your way, tell His disciples *and Peter.*"
What I wish you to notice here are the two
words, "and Peter." Why "and Peter?" Was
not Peter one of the disciples? Surely he was,
the very head of the apostolic company. Why
then "and Peter"? No explanation is vouch-
safed in the text, but reflection shows that it was
the utterance of love towards the despondent,
despairing disciple, who had thrice denied his
Lord. If the message had simply been to the
disciples, Peter would have said, "Yes, I was
once a disciple, but I can no longer be counted

such; I thrice denied my Lord on that awful night with oaths and cursings; it doesn't mean me," but our tender, compassionate Lord through His angelic messengers sends the message, "Go, tell His disciples, and whoever you tell, be sure you tell poor, weak, faltering, broken-hearted Peter." Is this made up, or is this a real picture of our Lord? I pity the man so dull that he can imagine that this is fiction. Incidentally let it be noticed that this is recorded only in the Gospel of Mark, which, as is well known, is Peter's Gospel. As Peter dictated to Mark what he should record, with tearful eyes and grateful heart he would turn to him and say, "Mark, be sure you put that in, 'Tell His disciples *and Peter.*'"

Turn now to John xx. 27-29: "Then saith He to Thomas, Reach hither thy finger, and behold My hands; and reach hither thy hand, and thrust it into My side: and be not faithless, but believing. And Thomas answered and said unto Him, My Lord and my God. Jesus saith unto him, Thomas, because thou hast seen Me, thou has believed: blessed are they that have not seen, and yet have believed." Note here both the action of Thomas and the rebuke of Jesus. Each is too characteristic to be attributed to the art of some master of fiction. Thomas had not been with the disciples at the first appearance of our Lord. A week has passed by, another Lord's Day has come. This time Thomas makes sure of being present; if the Lord is to appear he will be there. If he had been like some modern skeptics he would have taken pains to be away, but doubter though he was, he was an honest doubter, and wanted to know. Suddenly Jesus stands in the midst. He says to Thomas, "Reach hither thy finger, and behold My hands; and reach hither thy hand, and thrust it into My side: and be not faithless, but believing." Thomas' eyes are opened at last. His faith long dammed back bursts every barrier, and sweeping on carries Thomas to a higher height than any other disciple had gone yet—exultingly and adoringly he cries, as he looks up into the face of Jesus, "My Lord and my God." Then Jesus tenderly, but oh, how searchingly, rebukes him. "Thomas," He says, "because thou hast seen Me, thou hast believed: blessed are they" (who are so eager to find and so quick to see and so ready to accept the truth that they do not wait for ocular demonstration, but are ready to take truth on sufficient testimony) "that have not seen, and yet have believed." Is this made up, or is this life? A record of facts as they occurred or a fictitious production of some master artist?

Turn now to John xxi. 21, 22: "Peter seeing him saith to Jesus, Lord, and what shall this man do? Jesus saith unto him, If I will that he tarry till I come, what is that to thee? follow thou Me." Let us get the setting of these words. The disciples are on the beach of Galilee, breakfast is over, Jesus has told Peter how he is to glorify Him in a martyr's death. Jesus then starts to walk down the beach, and says to Peter, " Follow Me." Peter starts out to follow, but looking back over his shoulder to see what others were doing he sees John also following. With characteristic curiosity he says, " Lord, if I am to die for Thee, what shall this man do?" Jesus never answered questions of mere speculative curiosity regarding others, but pointed the questioner to his own duty. On another occasion (Luke xiii. 23, 24), when one came to Him with the question, " Are they few that be saved?" He replied to the question by telling them to see that they are saved themselves. So now He points curious Peter away from questions that do not concern him regarding others to his own immediate duty. He says, " If I will that he tarry till I come, what is that to thee? follow thou Me." Is this made up, or is this life and reality?

Turn to other verses in the same chapter, John xxi. 15-17: " So when they had dined, Jesus saith to Simon Peter, Simon, son of Jonas, lovest thou Me more than these? He saith unto Him, Yea, Lord; Thou knowest that I love Thee. He saith unto him, Feed My lambs. He saith to him again the second time, Simon, son of Jonas, lovest thou Me? He saith unto Him, Yea, Lord; Thou knowest that I love Thee. He

saith unto him, Feed My sheep. He saith unto
him the third time, Simon, son of Jonas, lovest
thou Me? Peter was grieved because He said
unto him the third time, Lovest thou Me? And
he said unto Him, Lord, Thou knowest all
things; Thou knowest that I love Thee. Jesus
saith unto him, Feed My sheep." What I wish
you to note especially here are the words, " Peter
was grieved because He said unto him the third
time, Lovest thou Me? " Why did Jesus ask
Peter three times " Lovest thou Me? " And
why was Peter grieved because Jesus did ask
him three times. We are not told in the text,
but if we read it in the light of Peter's thrice-
repeated, threefold denial of His Lord, we will
understand it. As Peter had denied his Lord
thrice, Jesus three times gives Peter an oppor-
tunity to reassert his love, but this all, tender as
it was, brings back to Peter that awful night
when in the courtyard of Annas and Caiaphas
he had thrice denied his Lord, and Peter was
grieved because He said unto him the third time,
" Lovest thou Me? " Is this made up? Did
the writer make it up with this fact in view? If
he did, he surely would have mentioned it. No,
this is no fiction, this is simply reporting what
actually occurred. The accurate truthfulness of
the record comes out even more strikingly in the
Greek than in the English version. Two different words are used for love. Jesus, in asking
Peter " Lovest thou Me? " uses a strong word

of a higher form of love. Peter replying, "Lord, Thou knowest I love Thee," uses a weaker word, but a more tender word (I am fond of Thee). Jesus the second time uses the stronger word, "Lovest thou Me?" and a second time Peter replies, using the weaker word. In His third question Jesus comes down to Peter's level, and uses the weaker word that Peter had used, and Peter replies, "Lord, Thou knowest all things; Thou knowest that I love Thee," using the same weaker word.

Notice again the appropriateness of the way in which Jesus revealed Himself to different persons after His resurrection. To Mary He reveals Himself simply by calling her by name. Read John xx. 16, "Jesus saith unto her, Mary. She turned herself and saith unto Him, Rabboni; which is to say, Master." What a delicate touch of nature we have here. Mary, as we saw a few moments ago, is standing outside the tomb overcome with grief. She has not recognized her Lord, though He has spoken to her; she has mistaken Him for the gardener. She has said, "Sir, if thou hast borne Him hence, tell me where thou hast laid Him, and I will take Him away." Then Jesus utters just one word; He says, "Mary." As that name came trembling on the morning air, uttered with the old familiar tone, spoken as no one else had ever spoken it but He, in an instant her eyes are opened, she falls at His feet and tries to clasp them, and looks up into His face and cries, "Rabboni; my Master." Is that made up? No, this is life, this is Jesus, and this is the woman who loved Him. No unknown author of the second, third or fourth century has produced such a masterpiece as this. We stand here unquestionably face to face with reality, with life, with Jesus and Mary, as they actually were.

To the two on the road to Emmaus He made Himself known in the breaking of bread. Read Luke xxiv. 30, 31, "And it came to pass, as He sat at meat with them, He took bread, and blessed it, and brake, and gave to them. And their eyes were opened, and they knew Him: and He vanished out of their sight." They knew Him in the breaking of bread. Why? The evangelist ventures no explanation, but it is not hard to read between the lines and find the explanation. In each one of the Gospels emphatic mention is made of Jesus returning thanks at meals. There was something so characteristic in the way He returned thanks at meals, so real, so different from the way in which they had ever seen any other man do it, there was such an evident approach into the very presence of God so utterly unlike the formality and unreality of others at such a time, that the moment Jesus lifted up His eyes and gave thanks, their eyes were opened —and they knew Him. This too is reality and life, not fiction.

To Thomas, the man governed by the senses, He made Himself known by exhibiting the very print of the nails in His hands and the hole in His side. To John and Peter, He made Himself known as at the beginning in the miraculous draught of fishes. Everywhere in each minute detail the narrative has a consistency and a truth to life that makes the supposition of fiction impossible.

Take one more illustration. Read carefully John xx. 7, "And the napkin that was about His head, not lying with the linen clothes, but wrapped together in a place by itself." How strange that such a little detail as this should be added to the story with absolutely no attempt of saying why, but how deeply significant this little unexplained detail is. When I was studying in the theological seminary an upper classman came home one Sunday afternoon from his Bible class much disgusted. He had a class of working girls about twenty years of age. He said, "One of my scholars asked me a stupid question to-day; she asked me if there was any significance in the napkin being wrapped together in a place by itself. How stupid, as if there was any significance in that!" But in reality it was not stupid working girl, but stupid theologue. There is the deepest significance in it. Jesus Christ is dead. For three days and three nights, from Wednesday evening at sunset till Saturday evening at sunset, His body has lain cold and silent in the sepulcher, as truly dead as any body was ever dead, but at last the appointed hour has come, the breath of God sweeps through the sleeping and silent clay, and in that supreme moment of His own earthly life, that supreme moment of human history, when Jesus rises triumphant over death and Satan, there is no excitement upon His part, but with that same majestic self-composure and serenity that marked His whole career, the same divine calm that He displayed upon storm-tossed Galilee when His affrighted disciples shook Him from His slumbers and said, " Lord, carest Thou not that we perish? " and He arose serenely on the deck of the tossing vessel and said to the raging waves and winds, " Be still! " and there was a great calm, so now again in this sublime, this awful moment, He does not excitedly tear the napkin from His face and throw it aside, but absolutely without human haste or flurry or disorder, He takes it calmly from His head, rolls it up and lays it away in an orderly manner by itself. Was that made up? Never! Never! We do not behold here a delicate masterpiece of the romancer's art—we read here the simple narrative of a matchless detail in a unique life that was actually lived here upon earth, a life so exquisitely beautiful that one cannot read it with an honest and open mind without feeling the tears coming to his eyes.

But someone will say: " These are little

things." True, but it is from that very fact that they gain very much of their significance. It is in just such little things that the fiction would disclose itself. Fiction displays its difference from the fact in the minute. In the great outstanding outlines you can make fiction look like truth, but when you come to examine it minutely and microscopically you will soon detect that it is not reality, but fabrication; but the more microscopically we examine the Gospel narratives, the more we become impressed with their truthfulness. The artlessness and naturalness and self-evident truthfulness of the narratives down to the minutest detail surpasses all the possibilities of art.

In our next Talk we shall consider the circumstantial evidence for the resurrection of Christ.

SEVENTH TALK

In our last two addresses we have been consider-
ing some of the internal proofs of the truthfulness of the Gospel story. We started out without
assuming anything. We took the four Gospels
without assuming them to be true, or to have
been written by the men whose names they bear,
or to have been written in the first century, or
second, or third. We assumed nothing whatever, but simply laid the Gospels side by side to
see what we could learn from a consideration of
the documents themselves as to whether they
were the record of facts that actually occurred,
or fictions. We first discovered that the four
Gospels contained separate and independent accounts of the resurrection of Christ. We next
saw that these Gospel stories must be either a
record of facts that actually occurred, or else
fiction; that if fiction, they must have been fabricated in one of two ways—either independently
of one another, or in collusion with one another.
We saw that they could not have been fabricated
independently of one another, as the agreements

were too marked and too many. We saw that they could not have been fabricated in collusion, the apparent discrepancies were too numerous and too noticeable. Not fabricated independently, not fabricated in collusion, we were therefore driven to the conclusion that they were not fabricated at all, but a true record of facts that actually occurred. We saw, in the next place, that each one of the four Gospels bore the clear marks of having been derived from eye-witnesses. We noted, in the next place, the artlessness, straightforwardness, and simplicity of the narratives, the entire absence of all attempt at coloring or effect, the certain mark of a true witness. We noted, in the next place, that it is often the case when a witness is on the witness stand that the unintentional evidence of words and phrases which he uses, and accidental details which he introduces, is more conclusive than the direct testimony of the witness, because it is not the testimony of the witness, but the testimony of the truth to itself. We then took up a large number of instances of this kind, conclusively showing that the Gospel stories could not have been made up; that beyond a peradventure they were the accurate representation of things that actually occurred.

To-day we take up the circumstantial evidence for the resurrection of Christ. I presume you all know what is meant by circumstantial evidence. By circumstantial evidence we mean certain proven or admitted facts or circumstances which demand for their explanation the other fact which we are seeking to prove. For example, a man was once found murdered; the only clue to the murderer was the point of a knife-blade which was found broken off in the heart. With this clue the detectives went to work. A knife was found with a broken blade. The jagged edges of the broken blade fitted exactly into the notches in the point that had been found in the heart. Moreover, there were traces of blood upon both point and blade, and the traces of blood on the point fitted exactly the traces of blood on the blade. It was held to be proven that the murder was committed with that knife. Take another illustration. A bolt of cloth was stolen from a certain manufacturer; search was made for the bolt of cloth. A bolt of cloth was found, which the manufacturer claimed was his stolen bolt; but the man in whose possession the bolt was found claimed that the bolt came from an entirely different factory. But when the bolt of cloth was taken to the factory from which the bolt had been stolen, the holes at each end of the bolt of cloth fitted exactly upon the tenter-hooks of the factory from which it was alleged to have been stolen. But when it was taken to the factory from which the man claimed to have obtained it, it was found that the holes in the end of the bolt of cloth did not at all fit upon the tenter-hooks of that factory.

On this evidence it was held to be proven that the bolt of cloth had come from the factory where it fitted upon the tenter-hooks. There is abundant evidence of this character as to the certainty of the resurrection of Christ from the dead. There are certain proven and admitted facts that demand the resurrection of Christ to account for them.

(1) Beyond a question, the foundation truth preached in the early years of the Church's history was the resurrection. This was the one doctrine upon which the Apostles were ever ringing the changes. Whether Jesus did actually rise from the dead or not, it is certain that the one thing that the apostles constantly proclaimed was that He had risen.

Why should the Apostles use this as the very corner stone of their creed if not well attested and firmly believed? Furthermore, they laid down their lives for this doctrine. Men do not lay down their lives for a doctrine which they do not firmly believe. They stated that they had seen Jesus after His resurrection, and rather than give up their statement died for it. Of course, men may die for error, and often have; but in this case they would know whether they had seen Jesus or not, and they would not merely have been dying for error, but dying for a statement which they knew to be false. This is not credible. Furthermore, if the Apostles really firmly believed, as is admitted, that Jesus rose from the dead, they had some facts upon which they founded their belief. These are the facts they would have related in recounting the story, and not have made up a story out of imaginary incidents. But if the facts were as recounted in the Gospels, there is no possible escaping the conclusion that Jesus actually arose.

Furthermore, if Jesus had not arisen, there would have been some evidence that He had not. His enemies would have found this evidence. But the Apostles went up and down the very city where He had been crucified and proclaimed right to the face of the slayers that He had been raised, and no one could produce evidence to the contrary. The best they could do was to say the guards went to sleep and the disciples stole the body while the guards slept. Men who bear evidence to what happens while they are asleep are hardly credible witnesses. Further still, if the Apostles had stolen the body, they would have known it themselves, and would not have been ready to die for what they knew to be a fraud.

(2) Another known fact is the change in the day of rest. The early Church came from among the Jews. From time immemorial the Jews had celebrated the seventh day of the week as their day of rest and worship; but we find the early Christians, in the Acts of the Apostles, and also in early Christian writings, assembling on the first day of the week. Nothing is harder than to change a holy day that has been celebrated for

centuries, and is one of the most cherished customs of the people. What is especially significant about the change is that it was changed by no express decree, but by general consent. Something tremendous must have happened that led to this change. The Apostles asserted that what had happened on that day was the resurrection of Christ from the dead, and that is the most rational explanation, in fact, the only reasonable explanation of the change.

(3) But the most significant fact of all is the change in the disciples—the moral transformation. At the time of the crucifixion of Christ we find the whole apostolic company filled with blank and utter despair. We see Peter, the leader of the apostolic company, denying his Lord three times with oaths and cursings. But a few days later we see this same man filled with a courage that nothing could shake. We see Peter standing before the very council that had condemned Jesus to death, and saying to them: " Be it known unto you all, and to all the people of Israel, that in the name of Jesus of Nazareth, whom ye crucified, whom God raised from the dead, doth this man stand before you whole " (Acts iv. 10). A little further on, when commanded by this council not to speak at all nor teach in the name of Jesus, we hear Peter and John answering: " Whether it be right in the sight of God to hearken unto you more than unto God, judge ye. For we cannot but speak

the things which we have seen and heard"
(Acts iv. 19, 20). A little later still, after arrest
and imprisonment, in peril of death, when
sternly arraigned by the council, we hear Peter
and the other Apostles answering their demand
that they should be silent regarding Jesus: "We
ought to obey God rather than man. The God
of our Fathers raised up Jesus whom ye slew
and hanged on a tree. Him hath God exalted
with His right hand to be a Prince and a Saviour, and we are His witnesses of these things"
(Acts v. 29, 32). Something tremendous must
have happened to account for such a radical and
astounding moral transformation as this. Nothing short of the fact of the resurrection, of their
having seen the risen Lord, will explain it.

These unquestionable facts are so impressive
and so conclusive that even infidel and Jewish
scholars now admit that the Apostles believed
that Jesus rose from the dead. Even Ferdinand
Baur admits this. Even David Strauss says:
"Only this much need be acknowledged, that
the Apostles firmly believed that Jesus had
arisen." Strauss evidently does not wish to admit any more than he has to, but he feels com-
pelled to admit this much. Schenkel goes further yet, and says: "It is an indisputable fact
that in the early morning of the first day of the
week following the crucifixion the grave of Jesus
was found empty. It is a second fact that the
disciples and other members of the apostolic

communion were convinced that Jesus was seen after the crucifixion." These admissions are fatal to the rationalists who make them. The question at once arises, Whence this conviction and belief? Renan attempts an answer by saying that "the passion of a hallucinated woman [Mary] gives to the world a resurrected God" (Renan's "Life of Jesus," p. 357). By this Renan means that Mary was in love with Jesus. After His crucifixion, brooding over it, in the passion of her love she dreamed herself into a condition where she had a hallucination that she had seen Jesus arisen from the dead; she reported her dream as fact, and thus the passion of a hallucinated woman gave to the world a resurrected God. But, we reply, the passion of a hallucinated woman was not competent to this task. Remember the make-up of the apostolic company. In the apostolic company were a Matthew and a Thomas to be convinced and a Saul outside to be converted. The passion of a hallucinated woman will not convince a stubborn unbeliever like Thomas, nor a Jewish tax-gatherer like Matthew. Who ever heard of a tax-gatherer, and, most of all, a Jewish tax-gatherer, who could be imposed upon by the passion of a hallucinated woman? Neither will the passion of a hallucinated woman convince a fierce and conscientious enemy like Saul of Tarsus. We must find some saner explanation than this.

Strauss tries to account for it by inquiring

whether the appearances might not have been
visionary. To this we reply that, first of all,
there was no subjective starting-point for such
visions. The Apostles, so far from expecting to
see the Lord, would scarcely believe their own
eyes when they did see Him. Furthermore, who
ever heard of eleven men having the same vision
at the same time, to say nothing of five hundred
men (I Cor. xv. 6) having the same vision at
the same time? Strauss demands of us that we
give up one miracle and substitute five hundred
miracles in its place. Nothing can surpass the
credulity of unbelief.

The third attempt at an explanation is that
Jesus was not really dead when they took Him
from the cross, that His friends worked over
Him and brought Him back to life, and what
was supposed to be the appearance of the risen
Lord was the appearance of one who had never
been really dead, but only apparently dead, and
was now merely resuscitated. To sustain this
view appeal has been made to the short time
Jesus hung upon the cross, and to the fact that
history tells us of one in the time of Josephus
taken down from the cross and nursed back to
life. But to this we answer, first, remember the
events that preceded the crucifixion, the agony
in the garden of Gethsemane, the awful ordeal
of the four trials, the scourging, and the conse-
quent physical condition in which all this left
Jesus. Remember, too, the water and the blood

that poured from the pierced side. ' In the second place, we reply, His enemies would have taken, and did take, all necessary precautions against such a thing as this happening (John xix. 34). We reply, in the third place, if Jesus had been merely resuscitated, He would have been so weak, such an utter physical wreck, that His reappearance would have been measured at its real value, and the moral transformation in the disciples, for which we are trying to account, would still remain unaccounted for. The officer in the time of Josephus, who is cited in proof, though brought back to life, was an utter physical wreck. We reply, in the fourth place, if brought back to life, the Apostles and friends of Jesus, who are the ones who are supposed to have brought Him back to life, would have known how they brought Him back to life, and that it was not a case of resurrection, but of resuscitation, and the main fact to be accounted for, namely, the change in themselves, would remain unaccounted for. The attempted explanation is an explanation that does not explain. We reply, in the fifth place, that the moral difficulty is the greatest of all. If it was merely a case of resuscitation, then Jesus tried to palm Himself off as one risen from the dead, when He was nothing of the sort; He was an arch-imposter, and the whole Christian system rests on a fraud as its ultimate foundation. Is it possible to believe that such a system of religion as that of Jesus Christ, embodying such

exalted precepts and principles of truth, purity,
and love, "originated in a deliberately planned
fraud"? No one whose own heart is not cankered by fraud and trickery can believe Jesus to
have been an impostor, and His religion to have
been founded upon fraud.

We have eliminated all other possible suppo-
sitions. We have but one left, namely, Jesus
really was raised from the dead the third day
as is recorded in the Gospels. The desperate
straits to which those who attempt to deny it are
driven are themselves proof of the fact.

We have then several independent lines of argument pointing decisively to the resurrection of
Christ from the dead. Some of these taken sep-
arately prove the fact, but taken together they
constitute an argument that makes doubt of the
resurrection of Christ impossible to the candid
man. Of course, if one is determined not to
believe, no amount of proof will convince. Such
a man must be left to his own deliberate choice
of error and falsehood, but any man who really
desires to know the truth and is willing to obey
it at any cost, must accept the resurrection of
Christ as a historically proven fact.

There is really but one weighty objection to
the doctrine that Christ arose from the dead, that
is, that "there is no conclusive evidence that any
other ever arose." To this a sufficient answer
would be, even if it were certain that no other
ever arose, it would not at all prove that Jesus

did not rise; for the life of Jesus was unique, His nature was unique, His character was unique, His mission was unique, His history was unique, and it is not to be wondered at, but rather to be expected, that the issue of such a life should also be unique. After all, this objection is simply David Hume's exploded argument against the possibility of the miraculous revamped. According to this argument, no amount of evidence can prove a miracle, because miracles are contrary to all experience. But are miracles contrary to all experience? To start out by saying that they are is to beg the very question at issue. They may be outside of your experience and mine; they may be outside the experience of this entire generation, but your experience and mine and the experience of this entire generation is not all experience. Every student of geology and astronomy knows that things have occurred in the past which are entirely outside the experience of the present generation. Things have occurred within the last four years that are entirely outside the experience of the fifty years preceding. True science does not start out with an *a priori* hypothesis that certain things are impossible. It simply studies the evidence to know what has actually occurred. It does not twist its observed facts to make them accord with *a priori* theories, but seeks to make its theories accord with facts as observed. To say that miracles are impossible and that no amount of evidence can therefore prove a miracle is to be supremely unscientific. Within the past few years in the domain of chemistry, for example, discoveries have been made regarding radium which seemed to run counter to all previous observations regarding chemical elements and to well-established chemical theories, but the scientist has not therefore said that these discoveries about radium cannot be true. He has rather gone to work to find out where the trouble was in his previous theories. The observed and recorded facts in the case before us prove that Jesus rose from the dead, and true science must accept this conclusion and conform its theories to this observed fact.

In the day of the great triumph of Deism in England two of the most brilliant men in the denial of the supernatural were the eminent legal authorities, Gilbert West and Lord Lyttleton. These two men, who were put forward to crush the defenders of the supernatural in the Bible, had a conference together. One of them said to the other that it would be difficult to maintain their position unless they disposed of two of the alleged bulwarks of Christianity, namely, the alleged resurrection of Jesus from the dead and the alleged conversion of Saul of Tarsus. Lyttleton undertook to write a book to show that Saul of Tarsus was never converted as is recorded in the Acts of the Apostles, but that his alleged conversion was a myth, if Gilbert West would write another book to show that the alleged resurrection of Christ from the dead was a myth. West said to Lyttleton: " I shall have to depend upon you for my facts, for I am somewhat rusty in the Bible," to which Lyttleton replied that he was counting upon West, for he too was somewhat rusty in the Bible. One of them said to the other: " If we are to be honest in the matter, we ought at least to study the evidence," and this they undertook to do. They had numerous conferences together while they were preparing their works. In one of these conferences West said to Lyttleton that there had been something on his mind for some time that he thought he ought to speak to him about, that as he had been studying the evidence he was beginning to feel that there was something in it. Lyttleton replied that he was glad that he had spoken about it so, for he himself was somewhat shaken, as he had been studying the evidence for the conversion of Saul of Tarsus. Finally, when the books were finished and the two men met, West said to Lyttleton: " Have you written your book?" He replied that he had, but he said: " West, as I have been studying the evidence and weighing it by the recognized laws of legal evidence, I have become satisfied that Saul of Tarsus was converted as is stated in the Acts of the Apostles, and that Christianity is true, and I have written my book on that side." The book can be found to-day in first-class libraries.

" Well," said West, " as I have studied the evidence for the resurrection of Jesus Christ from the dead, and have weighed it according to the acknowledged laws of evidence, I have become satisfied that Jesus really rose from the dead as recorded in the Gospels, and have written my book on that side." This book also can be found in our libraries to-day. Let any man of legal mind, any man who is accustomed and competent to weigh evidence, yes, any man with fair reasoning powers, and, above all, with perfect candor, sit down to the study of the facts regarding the resurrection of Jesus Christ from the dead, and he will become satisfied that beyond a peradventure Jesus rose from the dead as is recorded in the Gospels. But supppose He did rise from the dead, what of it? We will take that question up in our next address.

EIGHTH TALK

IN our last three addresses we have seen conclusive evidence that Jesus Christ rose from the
dead. We have followed a number of independent lines of argument. Several of these
taken alone satisfactorily prove the fact of the
resurrection, but taken together they constitute
an argument that makes doubt of the resurrection of Christ impossible to a candid mind. But
suppose He did rise from the dead, what of it?
What does His resurrection prove? It proves
everything that most needs to be proved. It
proves everything that is essential in Christianity.

1. First of all, *the resurrection of Christ from
the dead proves that there is a God, and that the
God of the Bible is the true God.* Every effect
must have an adequate cause, and the only adequate cause that will account for the resurrection of Jesus Christ is God, the God of the Bible.
When Jesus was here upon earth, He proclaimed
the God of the Bible "the God of Abraham,
Isaac, and Jacob," the God of the Old Testament
as well as the New. He claimed that after men
had put Him to death the God of Abraham,

101

Isaac, and Jacob, the God of the Bible, would raise Him from the dead the third day. This was a stupendous claim to make, apparently an absurd claim. For centuries men had come and gone; they had lived and died, and as far as human observation went, that was the end of them; but Jesus claimed that after all these centuries of men living, dying, and passing into oblivion, that God, the God of the Bible, would raise Him from the dead. Jesus died; He was crucified, dead, and buried; the appointed hour at which he had claimed God would raise Him from the dead came. God did raise Him from the dead, and thereby Jesus' astounding claim was substantiated, and it was decisively proven that there is a God, and that the God of the Bible is the true God. For centuries men have been seeking for proofs of the existence and character of God. There is the teleological argument, the argument from the marks of creative intelligence and design in the material universe; a good argument in its place. There is the argument from the intelligent guiding hand of God in human history; the ontological argument, and other arguments, all more or less convincing; but the resurrection of Jesus Christ from the dead provides us with a solid, scientific foundation for our faith in God. In the light of the resurrection our faith in God is built upon observed facts. In the light of the resurrection of Jesus atheism and agnosticism have no longer any standing ground. Well might Peter say, " We through Him are believers in God, who raised Him from the dead, and gave Him glory " (I Pet. i. 21). My belief in the God of the Bible is not a felicitous fancy. It is a fixed faith resting upon an incontrovertibly firm fact.

2. In the second place, *the resurrection of Jesus Christ from the dead proves that Jesus is a teacher sent from God, who received His message from God, that He was absolutely inerrant, that He spoke the very words of God.* This was Jesus' claim for Himself. In John vii. 16 He says, " My teaching is not Mine, but His that sent Me." In John xii. 49 He says, " I have not spoke of Myself; but the Father which sent Me, He gave me a commandment, what I should say, and what I should speak." In John xiv. 10, 11 He says, " Believest thou not that I am in the Father, and the Father in me? the words that I speak unto you I speak not of Myself: but the Father that dwelleth in Me, He doeth the works. Believe Me that I am in the Father, and the Father in Me: or else believe Me for the very works' sake." In John xiv. 24 He says, " The word which ye hear is not mine, but the Father's which sent Me." His claim was that His words were the very words of God. This, too, was a stupendous claim to make. Others have made similar claims, but the difference between their claims and that of Jesus is that Jesus substantiated His claim, and no one

else has ever substantiated his. God Himself
unmistakably set His seal upon this astounding
claim of Jesus Christ by raising Him from the
dead. In the light of the resurrection of Jesus
Christ from the dead, that school of criticism
that assumes to question the absolute inerrancy
of Jesus Christ as a teacher, and to set its authority up above that of Jesus, has absolutely
no standing ground. Yea, further, that school
of criticism, by putting forward its unsubstantiated claims in opposition to the demonstrated
claims of Jesus Christ, makes itself a laughing-
stock in the eyes of thoughtful men.

3. In the third place, *the resurrection of
Jesus Christ from the dead proves that He is
the Son of God.* The Apostle Paul says, in
Rom. i. 4, that He is " declared to be the Son
of God with power by the resurrection from the
dead," and anyone who will stop to think will
see that this is beyond a peradventure true.
When Jesus was here upon earth He claimed to
be divine in a sense in which no other man was
divine. He taught that while even the greatest
of God's prophets were only servants, He was
a Son, an only Son (Mark xii. 6, note context).
He claimed that He and the Father were one
(John x. 30), and that all men should honor
Him, even as they honored the Father (John v.
23); that He was so completely and fully in-
dwelt of God, such a perfect and absolute incar-
nation of God, that he that had seen Him had

seen the Father (John xiv. 9). This was a most
amazing claim to make, a claim which, if not
true, was rankest blasphemy. He told men that
they would put Him to death for making this
claim, but that after they had put Him to death
God Himself would set His seal to the claim by
raising Him from the dead. They did put Him to
death for making this claim; the disbelievers in
the deity of Jesus Christ of that day caused Him
to be nailed to the cross of Calvary for claiming
to be divine (Matt. xxvi. 63-66) ; but when the
appointed hour had come the breath of God
swept through the sleeping clay, and God Himself, as Jesus claimed He would, set His seal
to Christ's assertion of His own deity by raising
Him from the dead, and God thus proclaimed to
all ages, with clearer voice than if He should
speak from the open heavens to-day, " This is
My only-begotten Son, the One in whom I dwell
in all My fullness, so that he that hath seen Him
hath seen the Father." In the light of the resurrection of Jesus Christ from the dead Unitarianism has absolutely no logical standing ground.

4. In the fourth place, *the resurrection of Jesus
Christ from the dead proves that there is a judgment day coming.* On Mars Hill Paul declared
" God hath appointed a day in which He will
judge the world in righteousness by that Man
whom He hath ordained, whereof He hath given
assurance unto all men in that He hath raised
Him from the dead," thus making the resurrec-

tion of Christ the God-given assurance of the
coming judgment. But how does the resurrection of Christ give assurance of coming judgment? When Jesus was upon earth, He declared
that the Father had committed all judgment unto
Him. He declared further that the hour was
coming in which all that were in their graves
should hear His voice and come forth; they that
that had done good unto the resurrection of life,
and they that had done evil unto the resurrection
of judgment (John v. 22, 28, 29). Men ridi-
culed His claim, hated Him for making the claim,
put Him to death for making the claim, and the
other claim involved in it, that of deity, but God
set His seal to the claim by raising him from the
dead. The resurrection of Jesus Christ from
the dead, which is an absolutely certain fact of
history in the past, points with unerring finger
to an absolutely certain coming judgment in the
future. Belief in a coming judgment day is
no guess of theologians. It is a positive faith
founded upon a proven fact. In the light of
the resurrection of Jesus Christ from the dead
the man who continues in sin, flattering himself
with the hope that there will be no future day of
reckoning and of judgment, is guilty of madness.
Jesus will sit in judgment, and everyone of us
must give account to Him of the deeds done in
the body.

5. In the fifth place, *the resurrection of Jesus
Christ from the dead proves that every believer*

in Christ is justified from all things. We read
in Rom. iv. 25 (R. V.) that Jesus "was delivered up for our trespasses, and was raised for
our justification." More literally, " He was delivered up because of our trespasses (that is,
because we had trespassed), and was raised because of our justification (that is, because we
were justified)." The resurrection of Jesus
Christ proves decisively that the believer in Him
is justified. But how? When Jesus was on
earth He said that He would offer up His life a
ransom for many (Matt. xx. 28). The hour
came, He offered up His life on the cross of Calvary as a ransom for us. Now the atonement
has been made, but there still remains a question,
" Will God accept the atonement which has thus
been offered?" For three nights and three days
this question remains unanswered. Jesus lies in
the grave, cold and dead. The long predicted
hour comes, the breath of God sweeps through
that sleeping clay, and Christ rises triumphant
from the dead and is exalted to the right hand
of the Father, and God proclaims to the whole
universe, " I have accepted the atonement which
Jesus made." When Jesus died, He died as my
representative, and I died in Him; when He
arose, He rose as my representative, and I arose
in Him; when He ascended up on high and took
His place at the right hand of the Father in the
glory, He ascended as my representative and I
ascended in Him, and to-day I am seated in

Christ with God in the heavenlies. I look at
the cross of Christ, and I know that atonement
has been made for my sins; I look at the open
sepulcher and the risen and ascended Lord, and
I know that the atonement has been accepted.
There no longer remains a single sin on me, no
matter how many or how great my sins may
have been. My sins may have been as high as
the mountains, but in the light of the resurrection the atonement that covers them is as high
as heaven. My sins may have been as deep as
the ocean, but in the light of the resurrection the
atonement that swallows them up is as deep as
eternity. "Be it known unto you therefore,
brethren, that through this Man is proclaimed
unto you remission of sins, and by Him every
one that believeth is justified from all things."

6. In the sixth place, *the resurrection of
Jesus Christ from the dead proves that all who
are united to Christ by a living faith shall live
again.* Paul says, " If we believe that Jesus died
and rose again, even so them also which sleep
in Jesus will God bring with Him " (I Thess.
iv. 14). The believer is so united to Christ by
a living faith that if Christ rose, we must. If
the grave could not hold Him, it cannot hold us.
For centuries men have been seeking proofs of
immortality; we have had the dreams of poets
and the speculations of philosophers to cheer us
with the hope that we shall live again, but the
best of philosophical arguments only point to

the probability of a future life. In a matter like this, the human heart craves and demands something more than a probability. In the resurrection of Jesus Christ from the dead we get something more than probability—we get absolute certainty; we get scientific demonstration of life beyond the grave. The resurrection of Jesus Christ removes the hope of immortality from the domain of the speculative and the probable into the domain of the scientifically demonstrated and certain. We know there is a life beyond the grave.

A popular preacher has recently said, " Not a few are not at all sure that there is any life beyond the grave. They wish it could be proven. So do I. But we can do no more than infer it from the moral constitution of the universe." Thank God, this popular preacher is wrong. Before the resurrection of Jesus Christ, perhaps, we could " do no more than infer it from the moral constitution of the universe," but in the light of the resurrection it is no longer left to uncertain inferences from the moral constitution of the universe, it is proven. No further proof is needed. It is scientifically demonstrated, and to anyone who will candidly ponder the facts regarding the resurrection of Christ, unbelief or agnosticism in regard to the future life becomes an impossibility. In the light of the first Easter morning I go out into the cemeteries where lies the sleeping dust of father and mother, brother,

child, and all my tears are brushed away, for I
hear the Father saying, Thy father shall live
again; thy mother shall live again; thy brother
shall live again; thy child shall live again.

7. In the seventh place, *the resurrection of
Jesus Christ from the dead proves that it is the
believer's privilege to have daily, hourly, con-
stant victory over sin.* We are united not only
to the Lord who died, and thus made atonement for our sin, and thus delivered us from
the guilt of sin; we are united to the Lord who
rose again, who " ever liveth to make interces-
sion for us," and who has power to save to the
uttermost, power to keep us from falling day by
day, and to present us faultless before the presence of His glory with exceeding joy (Heb. vii.
25; Jude 24). I may be weak, utterly weak,
unable to resist temptation for a single hour, but
He is strong, infinitely strong, and He lives
to give me help and deliverance every day and
every hour. The question of victory over sin
is not a question of my weakness, but of His
strength, His resurrection power, always at my
disposal. He has all power in heaven and on
earth, and what my risen Lord has belongs to
me also. In the light of the resurrection of
Jesus Christ from the dead, failure in daily living
is unnecessary and inexcusable. In His resurrection life and power it is our privilege and our
duty to lead victorious lives. Four men were
once climbing up the slippery side of the Matter-

horn, a guide and a tourist, a second guide and a second tourist, all roped together. The lower tourist lost his footing and went over the side. The sudden pull on the rope carried the lower guide with him, and he carried the other tourist with him. Three men are now dangling over the dizzy cliff. But the guide who was in the lead, feeling the first pull upon the rope, drove his pike into the ice, braced his feet, and held fast; three men dangling over the awful abyss, but three men safe, because tied to the man that held fast. The first tourist regained his place upon the path, the guide regained his, and the lower tourist regained his, and on and up they went in safety. As the human race ascended the icy cliffs of life, the first Adam lost his footing and swept over the abyss. He pulled the next man after him, and the next, and the next, and the next, until the whole race hung over the abyss; but the second Adam, the Man in the glory, stood fast, and all who are united to Him by a living faith, though dangling over the awful precipice, are safe, because tied to the Man in the glory.

NINTH TALK

INFIDELITY : ITS CAUSES, CONSEQUENCES, AND
CURE

THE profession of infidelity is very common in
our day. I am constantly meeting with those
who give as their reason for not being Christians that they do not believe in the Bible. There
are many preachers, most excellent and gifted
men, who think that infidelity is not worthy of
attention, that the proper way to treat it is to
ignore it. I do not agree with them. Infidelity
is common enough, and active enough, and destructive enough to demand attention. While I
do not for a moment think that the cause of
Christ or the Bible has anything to fear from
infidelity, I do know that individuals and com-
munities are being greatly injured by it, and we
owe it to them to expose its real character,
to point out its consequences, and to show its
cure.

I have had no greater joy now for some years
than to be able to lead many men out of the con-
fusion and wretchedness of infidelity into the
clear light and abounding joy of an intelligent
faith in Christ and the Bible.

I. Causes of Infidelity.

What are the causes of infidelity?

1. *The first cause, and one of the commonest, is misrepresentation of Christianity by its professed disciples.* There are two kinds of misrepresentations. (1) Misrepresentations in doctrine. (2) Misrepresentations in daily living. Let us look first at the misrepresentations in doctrine. Take, for example, what has been preached as Christianity for generations in France, Spain, Italy, the Philippine Islands, Mexico, and the South American republics. Of course we know that this is only the grossest caricature of the Christianity of the Bible; but the common people of these lands do not know this. They suppose that the Christianity preached by the priests is the Christianity of the Bible; and is it any wonder that they reject it and become out and out infidels? If what is thus preached as Christianity were Christianity, I would reject Christianity myself. But many so-called Protestant representations of Christianity, if not so grossly false, are still false. There is a wide difference between the God of the Bible and the God of much so-called Protestant teaching, between the Christ of the Bible and the Christ of much of the so-called Protestant teaching, and between the Christian life as set forth in the Bible and the ethics set forth in the pulpit. But the grossest

misrepresentation of Christianity on the part of its professed disciples are the misrepresentations in daily living. The life of many professed Christians is so widely at variance with the life taught in the Bible that it leads many observers into rank infidelity. Take, for example, the professed Christian who oppresses his employees in their wages. How many a professed Christian employer there is to-day who grinds his employees almost beyond endurance. Is it any wonder that these employees say that they have no use for Christianity? Look at the professed Christians in business who are dishonest in trade, who misrepresent their goods, who use all manner of dishonorable means to get ahead of their competitors in business and to drive them to the wall. Is it any wonder that people looking on are led to give up Christianity thus misrepresented? On one occasion, at the wedding of a young man in business in the city of Chicago, after the ceremony I began to speak to him about becoming a Christian, but he replied, " You need not talk to me about that. I work for ———— ————. These men are very prominent in the church, and we know how they carry on their business, as we are in their employ. I have no desire to be a Christian." Look at the professed Christian who rolls up his millions and lives in lavish luxury while the poor are starving at his doors. You may say to me that these misrepresentations of Christianity are no sufficient excuse for infidelity, that men and women ought to learn to distinguish between real Christianity and its counterfeit, and this I admit. Of course a really intelligent man never refuses good money because there is counterfeit money in circulation. But many men do not distinguish. They do not read the Bible for themselves, and their only idea of Christianity is from what they see in the lives and teachings of its professed disciples, and they say, " If that is Christianity, I do not want it," and so they become infidels. One of the most noted infidels of modern times claimed that it was the inconsistent living of his own father, who was a Baptist preacher, that first led him into infidelity. Whether his picture of his father's character is true or not, or whether to defend his own infidelity he was guilty of gross misrepresentation of his own father, as I have heard it alleged that he was, I cannot say, but this I do know, that beyond a question in many instances the inconsistencies of professedly Christian parents have led their children into utter infidelity. Misrepresentation of Christianity by its professed disciples in their teachings, and especially in their lives, has done more to manufacture infidels than all the writings and speeches that all the Paines and Voltaires and Ingersolls ever gave to the world.

2. *The second cause of infidelity is ignorance; ignorance of what the Bible contains and teaches, ignorance of history, and ignorance of*

true science. The average infidel knows almost
nothing about the Bible. He has caught up a
few difficulties here and there from the writings
or speeches of other infidels, but of the real con-
tents of the Bible he knows practically nothing.
I once asked a man if he would become a Christian; he replied, No, that he was an infidel.
" Why are you an infidel? " " Because the Bible
is so full of contradictions." " Well," I said,
" if the Bible is full of contradictions, please show
me one." " Why," he said, " it is full of them."
" If it is full of them, you ought at least be able
to show me one." " Why, it is full of them."
" Well, show me one." " Well, it is in the book
of Psalms." I handed him my Bible to find it,
and he began looking for the Psalms in the back
part of the New Testament. " Let me find the
Book of Psalms for you." When I found the
Psalms for him, he began to fumble around for
awhile, then he said, " If I had my Bible here I
could show it to you." " Will you bring your
Bible to-night and meet me here at the close of
the meeting? " He promised that he would.
The appointed hour came, and I was at the appointed place, but my infidel friend did not
appear. I had taken the precaution of taking
his address, and went to the address he had
given, and found it a public-house, but did not
find my man. Months afterwards, in one of our
after-meetings, one of my students called to me
and said, " Come here—here is a man who says

the Bible is full of contradictions." I went over, and behold it was the same man. The man evidently thought I would not recognize him, but I did, and said, " You are the man that lied to me." He dropped his head and said, " Yes." Another smart young infidel once said to me, " I don't believe the Bible." I asked him why not. He replied, " I don't believe that passage where it speaks about Christ calling down fire from heaven to destroy His enemies." When I assured him that there was no such passage in the Bible, he would not believe me. An infidel in Edinburgh asked me to explain the passage where it said, " Cain went into the land of Nod and *took to himself* a wife." When I said the Bible does not say so, he offered to bet me £100 that it did. Colonel Ingersoll, the high-priest of the cheaper and more superficial infidelity of the day, is an illustration of this ignorance of the Bible. He said in one of his lectures, " There is not a single kind and loving sentiment attributed to Christ but was uttered by Buddha at least 500 years before Christ was born." I would like to know where he finds any utterance of Buddha similar to John xiii. 34, "A new commandment I give unto you, That ye love one another; as I have loved you, that ye also love one another." Or John xv. 12, 13, " This is My commandment, That ye love one another, as I have loved you. Greater love hath no man than this, that a man lay down his life for his friends."

Or Matt. xx. 28, "Even as the Son of man
came not to be ministered unto, but to minister,
and to give His life a ransom for many." In
another place Colonel Ingersoll said, "If Christ
ever lived on the earth, He was an infidel in His
time." I would like to know what Colonel Ingersoll does with such statements as that of
John x. 35, "The Scripture cannot be broken";
or Matt. v. 18, "Till heaven and earth pass, one
jot or one tittle shall in no wise pass from the
law, till all be fulfilled." Or Mark vii. 13, where,
speaking of the law of Moses, He calls it the
Word of God. Or with Luke xxiv. 27, 44, "And
beginning at Moses and all the prophets, he expounded unto them in all the scriptures the
things concerning Himself. . . . And He said
unto them, These are the words which I spake
unto you, while I was yet with you, that all
things must be fulfilled which were written in
the law of Moses, and in the prophets, and in
the Psalms concerning Me." If this is infidelity,
then I am an infidel. But all intelligent men
know this is not infidelity, and that Colonel Ingersoll was simply parading his ignorance when
he uttered his statement. One of the leaders
of English infidelity some years ago in an article
in one of the secularist journals, spoke of Matthew as a "dispenser of liquors." He knew so
little of the Bible that he supposed the word
"publican" used of Matthew in the Bible meant
publican in the sense of a keeper of a public-

house. Perhaps the most prominent exponent
of materialistic infidelity among the Germans is
so ignorant of the historic discussions of Christian doctrine that he speaks of the virgin birth
of our Lord as " the immaculate conception ";
and one of the most prominent exponents of infidelity in England does the same thing.

3. *The third cause of infidelity is conceit.*
Many men tell us that they are infidels because
they find things in the Bible which they cannot
understand, and because there are in it apparent contradictions which they cannot reconcile.
To say that a thing cannot be true because I
cannot understand it, to think that God could
utter nothing that would be beyond my understanding, is the most consummate conceit. It is
to assume that I know all things, that I know as
much as God knows, and that therefore God
could not possibly utter anything that I could
not understand. To think that because I cannot
find the solution of a difficulty that therefore
none can be found, is to think that I know all
things, that my mind is infinite; it is to think that
I am God. Suppose I should take my little child
out about sunset, and say to the child, " Do you
see the sun yonder?" "Yes." "Well, my
child, that sun is over 92,000,000 miles away."
Then suppose the child should look up into my
face in her mature wisdom of nine years and say,
" Father, I know that is not true. The sun is
just behind the barn yonder." Would this be

a revelation of the child's wisdom, or its ignorance and conceit? The oldest, wisest philosopher compared with the Infinite is less than a child compared to the wisest of men; and for us to challenge our Father's statements, because they seem to us untrue, does not reveal us to be philosophers worthy of admiration and applause, but to be foolish children who ought to be sent to bed. If we find difficulties in the Bible that we cannot explain, a moderate degree of modesty on our part would lead us to say, " If I knew a little more, I might be able to readily explain this difficulty," rather than lead us to say, " This Book that contains a difficulty which I cannot explain surely cannot be from God." When in Birmingham, a man who parades his infidelity by having quotations from various infidels at the head of his note paper wrote me saying that the Bible could not be the Word of God, as it was full of contradictions; that he could send me hundreds of them, but one or two would suffice, as they could not be answered. The difficulties sent were very easy of solution, and I wrote him the solution; but instead of being staggered in his conviction that the difficulties he held were insoluble, he wrote that he was sorry that he had been so unfortunate in his choice of difficulties before, but would now send me some more. These were quite as easy of solution. But this did not seem to suggest to him that his other apparently unanswerable difficulties would be as

easy of solution as these formerly unanswerable
difficulties, if he only knew a little more.

4. *The fourth cause of infidelity is sin.* This
is the commonest and most fundamental cause
of infidelity. Sin causes infidelity in two ways;
first, men sin and betake themselves to infidelity
to find comfort in their sin. There is no book
that makes men so uneasy in sin as the Bible,
and if they can only make themselves believe
that the Bible is not true, it gives them some
solace in the pursuit of sin. Men tell you that
they have many objections to the Bible; but with
the great majority of them their greatest objection to the Bible, if they would confess the truth
to themselves and to others, is that it condemns
their sin, and makes them uneasy in their sin.
Second, sin blinds men's eyes to the truth of
the Bible, and makes it appear foolishness.
There is nothing that blinds the mind to truth
like sin. I was once called to deal with an infidel. I sat down, and he told me that the reason
that he could not be a Christian was because of
a difficulty he had with the Bible. I asked him
what his difficulty was. He replied that he could
not see where Cain got his wife. I said, " Will
you come to Christ if I tell you where Cain got his
wife?" "Oh," he said, "I will not promise
that." "But," I said, "if that is your difficulty
that keeps you from coming to Christ, and if
you are an honest man and I remove that difficulty, you will come to Christ." "No, I will

not promise that." I then went at the root of
the matter. I found out that his real difficulty
was not about Cain's wife at all, but about another man's wife. It is surprising how often
young men who fall into sin and into lax ways
of living fall also into infidelity. I have found
through conversation with young men who en-
tertain infidel views, that there are two specific
sins which are the commonest cause of unbelief.
My former colleague, Prof. W. W. White, was
speaking one time in Chicago on the " Mistakes
of Ingersoll." At the close of the lecture a fine-
looking man approached him and said, " Professor White, you have no right to say what you
have said to-day. You are a Christian, and I
am an infidel. I have just as much right to my
opinion as you have to yours." Professor White
then put to him a pointed question, " Is your life
pure?" The man replied, " That is none of
your business. My life is just as pure as yours
is." Then Professor White asked him his name.
The man said, " That is none of your business."
" But," said Professor White, " I want to look
up your record." The man declined to give it,
and began to back out. But there were those in
the company that gathered around that knew the
man's name, and gave it to Professor White.
Within two years from that time that man was
found dead in a Boston hotel, side by side with
a young woman, not his wife, whom he had be-
guiled into infidelity, and who had gone off with

him to lecture on infidelity. They were found dead together in this Boston hotel with the gas turned on. Gentlemen, the statement of this fact will make some of you angry, but look into your own hearts and lives and see if there is not some sin at the root of your infidelity. I do not say that all infidelity comes from sin, but I do say, after long and careful observation, that a very large share of the current infidelity of the day has sin for its ultimate cause.

5. *The fifth cause of infidelity is resistance to the Holy Spirit.* This is a very common cause of infidelity. The Spirit of God moves upon the hearts of men, inclining them to accept Christ. They will not yield to the Spirit of God. They resist the Holy Ghost, and the light which He gives to the soul is darkened, and they fall into skepticism or unbelief. In one of my pastorates there was a lawyer of excellent abilities, who was a most bitter opponent of Christianity, doing what he could to oppose it by bringing infidel lecturers to the town. I looked into this man's previous history. I found that there was a time in the very church of which I was pastor when he was under conviction of sin, and hesitating as to whether he should come out and accept Christ, and when pressed upon the subject he replied, " No, I cannot be a Christian and succeed in my business, and I must support my family." The light that was dawning upon his soul went out, and darkness and unbelief settled

down upon him, exercising such a blighting influence over his life that he lost the confidence
of his fellowmen, lost his law practice, and the
last I knew his wife was teaching school to help
support the family, while he was doing such odd
jobs as came to him.   In one of our western col-
leges there was a revival of religion.   Two
young men in the college set themselves against
it.   They were determined not to yield.   They
made an agreement together to meet on a certain evening and go into the chapel and blas-
pheme the Holy Ghost.   They met at the appointed hour, but the heart of one of the young
men failed him, and he was afterwards converted.   The other went into the college chapel
alone.   What he did in there no one knows, but
he came out white as a sheet.   He drifted into
infidelity, and became a leader in one of the secular societies in one of our large cities.   Oh,
you men who are resisting the Holy Spirit, if
we come back five years from now, we will most
likely find you infidels, and if we come back ten
years from now, in all probability we will find
you drunkards.   In the city of Melbourne more
than one man came to me, a moral wreck, who
said that his fall was due to the influence of the
noted infidel in that place.

In our next address we will take up the consequences and cure of infidelity.

TENTH TALK

In our last address we saw that the causes of infidelity were—first, misrepresentations of Christianity on the part of its professed adherents; second, ignorance of the Bible, and of history, and of science; third, conceit; fourth, sin; and fifth, resistance of the Holy Spirit.

We are to-day to take up the consequences and cure of infidelity.

II.   Consequences of Infidelity.

1. *The first consequence of infidelity is sin.* Infidelity breeds sin, there is no doubt of that. It is caused by sin, and in turn it begets a progeny like unto its ancestry. Sin first entered into human history through questioning God's Word. When the devil sought to lead Eve into disobedience to God, he began by throwing out an insinuation that the Word of God was not true. He first said, "Hath God said," and then he flatly denied what God said. The devil was the first infidel lecturer. He had an audience of but one, but he reached millions through that lecture. He saw at once the effectiveness of this

125

mode of attack upon man's moral integrity.
From that day to this the devil has been trapping
men into sin by sowing the seeds of unbelief in
their hearts.   He well knows what sort of a crop
that seed brings forth.   When a young man or a
young woman falls into infidelity, look out for
their morals.   Infidelity forms a very rickety foundation for an upright character.   A former Presi-
dent of the British National Secular Society, a
man well known here in Bolton, who in fact was
elected to Parliament from the Bolton district,
said, "I have seen the dreadful effects which
infidelity produces on men's characters; I have
had proof of its deteriorating effects in my own
experience; its tendency is to utter debasement."
Occupying the position that he did, Joseph
Barker certainly knew infidelity, and knew its
consequences, and this testimony of his to its
destructive effects upon character is beyond
question true.

   2. *The second consequence of infidelity is
anarchy.*   Anarchists are necessarily always infidels.   It is impossible for a man who believes
in the Bible to be an anarchist.   When the miserable French vagabond and anarchist Vaillant
stood upon the gallows, he boasted of his infidelity.   His infidelity and his anarchy went
hand in hand.   Louis Blanc, one of the great
leaders of anarchy, is reported to have said,
" When I was an infant I rebelled against my
nurse; when I was a child I rebelled against my

tutors and my parents; when I was a man I
rebelled against the Government; when I die,
if there is any heaven and I go there, I will rebel
against God." The acceptance of Christianity
would do away with anarchy on the one hand,
and it would do away with the oppression of the
poor by the rich that leads to anarchy on the
other hand.

3. *The third consequence of infidelity is
wretchedness and despair.* God has created us
for fullness of joy, and has made fullness of
joy possible for each one of us; but fullness of
joy such as God intends for man, and which
alone can satisfy a soul made in God's image,
can only come from a living faith in Jesus as the
Son of God, and in the Bible as the Word of
God. Infidels are never profoundly happy.
There may be surface joviality, but it is not, as
everyone knows who knows them well, deep and
satisfying. One night as I closed an address in
a New Zealand town a man somewhat beyond
middle life passed in front of the platform as he
made his way out of the building. He looked
up at me and scowled and said, "I am an infidel." I replied, "You do not need to tell us
that; your face shows it. You are one of the
most miserable-looking men I have ever seen."
I received a letter from him next day saying that
he was miserable. Did you ever know a joyous
old infidel? Jolly they may be, at least at times
when in company, but did you ever see that deep,

continuous, overflowing joyfulness that is so
characteristic of the aged Christian? On the
day of the death of a noted American infidel I
was with a friend of his, and we got to talking
about him. He said to me, " Every time of late
when I have gone to see him his wife has said
to me, ' Don't tell him that he is growing old; it
makes him very angry.' " But it does not make
the aged Christian angry to tell him he is growing old, for he knows he is but ripening for a
better world. Infidelity not infrequently begets
despair and suicide. Even the best of pagan
writers taught the propriety of suicide. For example, Epictetus says, " The door is open. When
you will you can leave off playing the game of
life." Mrs. Amelia E. Barr, who has made a
study of suicide, says, " The advent of Christianity made self-destruction a crime." She
further says that the infidel revival in France at
the time of the Revolution caused the abolition
of the civil and canon laws against suicide. She
still further says, " The great underlying cause
of the advance of modern suicide is the advance
of lax or skeptical religious views." Infidelity
leads logically to pessimism and despair. Ingersoll himself wrote an editorial in a New York
paper in defense of suicide. This editorial was
followed in New York and the neighborhood
by a harvest of suicides. The man who wrote
the editorial was directly responsible for its consequences, and it is not to be wondered at that

the editorial raised a storm of protest and indignation; but his article was the logical outcome of his infidelity. There came to Chicago at the time of the World's Fair a poor but brilliant young woman from one of the Southern States. Her intellectual gifts were so great that she was introduced into the best society, where she spoke upon the new woman. She was led into infidelity by an able advocate of unbelief in Chicago, but her career as an infidel was but brief. She soon met a suicide's death in an Eastern city, and one branch of the infidels of America to-day meet annually at her grave to commemorate her death. Her broken-hearted father also died by his own hand. Such is the legitimate fruit of unbelief.

4. *The fourth consequence of infidelity is a hopeless grave.* Colonel Ingersoll once said, " The pulpit has cast a shadow over the cradle and a gloom over the grave." If this is true, it is a most remarkable fact that people, even professedly infidel people, are so anxious to have Christian preachers conduct their funerals. There is a gloom over the grave by nature and by sin, but the Bible dispels the shadow. Throw away the Bible and you do not get rid of the gloom, but you do get rid of the light that illumines it. Infidelity shrouds the grave in gloom, and the only rays of light are those stolen from Christianity. Colonel Ingersoll, at his brother's grave, delivered an address, eloquent in words,

but sad beyond description. As he drew towards the close of that address he said that through the darkness hope sees the glimmering of a star; but he was not honest enough to say that that star was the Star of Bethlehem. On the other hand, D. L. Moody, at his brother's grave, sounded forth a note of joy and exultation. Looking into the grave he cried, "O death, where is thy sting? O grave, where is thy victory? The sting of death is sin; and the strength of sin is the law. But thanks be to God, which giveth us the victory through our Lord Jesus Christ."

Two men died the same year in America, Colonel Ingersoll, the acknowledged leader of American infidelity, and D. L. Moody, the leader of Christian activity. Compare the deaths and funerals of these two men, and see for yourselves whether the Christian's death or the infidel's is the gloomy one. The death of Colonel Ingersoll was sudden, and without a ray of cheer and brightness, his funeral unutterably pitiful. His wife and daughter, who loved him, could not bear to have the body taken from the house until the beginning of corruption made it an absolute necessity. It was all they had, and despairingly they clung to that body, now decaying. The scene at the crematory, as described in the daily papers, was enough to make the heart of any one ache, no matter how little one might be in sympathy with the views of the unfortunate man

who passed into eternity. On the other hand,
the death and funeral of Mr. Moody were triumphant in every detail. Early on the morning of
his departure from this world his eldest son was
sitting beside his bed. He heard his father
speaking in a low tone of voice, and he leaned
over to listen, and these were the words that he
heard: "Earth is receding; heaven is opening;
God is calling." "You are dreaming, father,"
said the son. "No, Will, this is no dream. I
have been within the gates. I have seen the
children's faces." The family were summoned.
Mr. Moody rallied. A while after he began to
sink again, and he was heard to say, "Is this
death? This is not bad; there is no valley. This
is bliss. This is glorious." "Father," said his
daughter, "you must not leave us. We cannot
spare you." The dying man replied: "I am not
going to throw my life away if God has any
more work for me to do, I will get well and do
it; but if God is calling, I must up and off." He
rallied again. He gained sufficient strength to
arise from the bed and walk over to the window,
and sat down in a chair and talked with his family. He began to think he would recover, and
was contemplating sending for his pastor to
pray for his recovery, but beginning to sink
again, he asked them to help him back to the bed.
As he was sinking his daughter knelt by the bed
and commenced to pray for his recovery, but he
said: "No, no, Emma, don't pray that. God

is calling. This is my coronation day. I have been looking forward to it," and the heroic warrior swept up into the presence of the King. At the funeral all was triumphant. His son said to me before the service: "Remember there is to be nothing of sadness in the service. We want nothing but triumph here to-day." The body was borne to the church by students from one of the schools that he had founded. It lay in an open casket in front of the pulpit. Right in front of it, with unveiled faces, sat his wife and daughter and sons listening with peaceful faces to the words that were spoken, and joining in the hymns of gladness and praise and victory. When others had ceased speaking, the eldest son arose and gladly gave testimony for his father and the power of his faith. Is it Christianity that throws a gloom over the grave? Is the Christian's grave the gloomy one, and the infidel's the bright one? Who ever heard of a Christian repenting on his deathbed that he had been a Christian? It is not at all uncommon for infidels to repent on their deathbed that they have been infidels.

5. *The fifth consequence of infidelity is eternal ruin.* We are told in Mark xvi. 16, " He that believeth and is baptized shall be saved, but he that believeth not shall be condemned." We are told in John iii. 36, " He that believeth in the Son hath everlasting life, but he that believeth not the Son shall not see life, but the wrath of

God abideth on him." We have all sinned, and
the only way to find pardon is by the acceptance
of the Sin-bearer whom God has provided. If
we prefer to be infidels and reject Him, there is
no hope. Jesus is **the** only Saviour who has
ever proved compet**ent** to save men from the
power of sin here, so we may rest assured He is
the only One who will prove competent to save
men from the consequences of sin hereafter. But
there are many who do not profess to be infidels,
who are not theoretically so, but are practically
so. All who reject Christ are practically infidels, and they will be lost. As Ethan Allen, a
brave soldier but hopeless infidel, stood at his
daughter's deathbed, she turned to him and
asked whether she should accept his unbelief or
her mother's faith, and the humbled man ad-
vised her to accept her mother's faith in that
trying hour.

III. THE CURE FOR INFIDELITY

We come now to the cure for infidelity.

1. *The great cure for infidelity is Christian
living on the part of professed Christians.*
There is no argument for Christianity like a
Christlike life. Many a skeptic and infidel has
been won by the life of one who not merely intel-
lectually believed in Christ, but who lived like
Him in his daily walk. McAll lay dead in his
coffin in Paris. A workman of Paris, a former

anarchist, stood by his coffin weeping. "Was
he a relative?" "No." "Why, then, do you
weep?" "He saved me." "What did he say?"
"He said nothing," replied the former anarchist,
"it was his face." The Christlike character
shining out in a Christlike countenance had saved
this man. I was once asked to call upon a woman
of brilliant gifts who was an unbeliever. "But,"
she said, "there is one thing I cannot get around,
that is my father's life." Not long after, by the
power of the truth as exemplified in her father's
life, leading her to a deeper study of the Bible,
she came out as an openly professed follower of
Jesus Christ.

2. *In the second place, the cure for infidelity is
a surrendered will on the part of the infidel.*
Jesus says, "Whosoever willeth to do His will,
he shall know of the teaching, whether it be of
God or whether I speak from myself" (John vii.
17, R.V.). Any man afflicted with the malady of
skepticism can find a remedy if he wishes it in
this simple prescription. Nothing so clarifies
the spiritual vision as a surrendered will. By
this simple act of the surrender of the will to
God many a man has found the mists of his unbelief scatter in a moment. When I was in New
Zealand a well-known and well-educated commercial traveler came to me and said: "My
friends wish me to speak to you. I am an agnostic, but I know that you cannot help me." I
told him that I thought that I could, but he was

sure that I could not. " What do you believe? "
I said. " I don't know as I believe anything."
" Do you not believe that there is an absolute difference between right and wrong? " " Yes, I do."
" Will you take your stand upon the right to follow it wherever it carries you? " " I think I am
doing that now." " Will you definitely here to-day
take your stand upon the right to follow it wherever it carries you, no matter what it costs? " He
said: " I will." " You do not know that God does
not answer prayer? " " No, I do not know that
God does not answer prayer." " Well, here is a
possible clue to knowledge. Will you follow it?
Will you pray this prayer? Oh God, if there is
any God, show me if Jesus Christ is Thy Son, and
if you show me that He is, I promise to accept
Him as my Saviour and confess Him before the
world? " " Yes," he said, " I will do that, but
it won't do any good." " Now John tells us in
John xx. 31, ' These are written, that ye might believe that Jesus is the Christ, the Son of God; and
that believing ye might have life through His
name.' Will you take the Gospel of John and
read it? Read carefully, slowly and thoughtfully.
Do not try to believe it nor do not try to disbelieve
it, simply be willing to be convinced of the truth.
Before you read kneel down and ask God to show
you what of truth there may be in the verses you
are about to read, and promise Him that whatever
He shows you to be true you will take your stand
upon." This he also agreed to do, parting from

me, assuring me that nothing would come.⌒
Some weeks after in Dunedin this man's w..
came to me and said: " I have had a letter from
my husband which I do not understand. He
said I might show it to you." In the letter he
said that he thought he was converted, but he
was not quite sure yet, that she could show this
letter to me and to the minister, but not to anyone else until he was perfectly sure of his position. He afterwards came out fully as a believer
in the Bible and in Christ.

3. *The third part of the cure for infidelity is
the study of the Word of God.* Men do not need
to study books of Christian evidences. The Bible
is its own best proof. Let any candid seeker
after the truth, anyone who sincerely desires to
know the truth, and is willing to obey it whatever it costs, get down to the earnest study of the
Bible, and he will soon become convinced that it
is the Word of God. In my first pastorate there
was a member of my church who had a brother a
lecturer on scientific subjects, but an infidel.
Sometimes he would lecture on the contradictions
between science and the Bible. She came to me
and asked if I would pray for him that he might
be converted. This I agreed to do. Some time
after this she came to me and said that her
brother had written her a letter, saying that he
had become a Christian. In this letter he gave
her the reason for his conversion. It was this:
" I have been recently studying the Bible, and

become convinced that it is the Word of ⊔od." It would have been well if he had studied the Bible before he lectured upon it and the contradictions between it and science.

In one of my pastorates I had a friend who lived across the street from me who was an agnostic. Though he was an agnostic and I a Christian minister, we were intimate friends, for I believe that a Christian and a Christian minister should rub up against all classes of men. I do not believe at all in the division of society into men, women, and ministers. I think a minister should be a man among men. How can we expect to influence men unless we touch elbows with them? Our Master was not too good to associate with all kinds and conditions of men, even the most depraved and outcast. Ought we to be better than our Master? I read in my Bible that Christians are the salt of the earth. How on earth can we expect the salt to exert its preservative influence upon the meat if we put the salt in one barrel and the meat in another? So I have always cultivated the friendship, not merely of orthodox Christians, but of all kinds of "heretics" and unbelievers. This man and I were good friends. We often met and talked together. One night we were standing together on his front lawn just as the sun went down, when he suddenly said: "Mr. Torrey, I am sixty-six years of age. I cannot live many more years. I have no one to leave my money to, and I cannot take it with me. I would give every penny of it if I could believe as you do." I replied: "That is very easy. I can tell you how." We went into the house, and I asked his wife for a sheet of paper, and I wrote upon it the following words: "I believe that there is an absolute difference between right and wrong" (I did not say I believe that there is a God, for this man was an agnostic, neither affirming nor denying the existence of God, and you have to begin where a man is), "and I hereby take my stand upon the right to follow it wherever it carries me. I promise to make an honest search to find if Jesus Christ is the Son of God, and if I find that He is, I promise to accept Him as my Saviour, and confess Him as such before the world." Having written this out, I handed it to my friend and said: "Will you sign that?" He replied: "Why, anybody ought to be willing to sign that. You only ask me to agree to do what my own conscience tells me I ought to do. Anybody ought to be willing to sign that." "Will you sign it?" I asked. "Why," he added more earnestly, "anybody ought to be willing to sign that." I said: "Will *you* sign it?" Still more earnestly he said: "Anybody ought to be willing to sign it." "Will you sign it?" "I will think about it," he said. He never signed it. He died as he had lived, without God, without Christ, without hope. He went out into the darkness of a Christless eternity. He told the truth about one thing. He

did not take one penny of his money with him.
They laid him in a Christless grave. He is now
in a Christless eternity, but whose fault was it?
A way was shown him out of darkness into light,
a way that he admitted his own conscience told
him he ought to take, and he would not take it.
Men, the same way has been shown to you. Follow it, and it will lead you as it has thousands of
others, out of the uncertainty and restlessness and
the ultimate despair of unbelief into the certi-
tude, the joy, the victory, and the ultimate glory
of an intelligent faith in the Bible as the Word
of God, and in Christ as the Son of God.

CPSIA information can be obtained at www.ICGtesting.com
Printed in the USA
BVOW03s1108161213

339265BV00015B/570/P